Grace
TO
STAND FIRM,
GRACE
TO GROW

D1114450

Light for Your Path

The Light for Your Path Series is for Christians who desire to know, love, and serve God better. Each book is designed to nurture new believers while challenging those who are ready for deeper study. Studies in the series examine *books* of the Bible, on the one hand (look for subtitles beginning with *Light from*), and important *topics* in Christian faith and life, on the other (look for subtitles beginning with *Focus on*). The series blends careful instruction with active reader participation in a variety of study exercises, always encouraging us to live in the light of biblical truth in practical ways.

Two foundational studies explain why and how to study the Bible as the one perfect light source for our Christian walk:

A Book Like No Other: What's So Special About the Bible
Turning On the Light: Discovering the Riches of God's Word

Also available:

The Light for Your Path Series Leader's Guide
God with Us: Light from the Gospels
Before the Throne of God: Focus on Prayer
His Witnesses to the World: Light from Acts
A Believer's Guide to Spiritual Fitness: Focus on His Strength

Grace TO STAND FIRM, GRACE TO GROW

LIGHT FROM 1–2 PETER

Carol J. Ruvolo

P&R
PUBLISHING
P.O. BOX 817 • PHILLIPSBURG • NEW JERSEY 08865-0817

Unless otherwise indicated, Scripture quotations are from the New American Standard Bible. Copyright by the Lockman Foundation 1960, 1962, 1963, 1968, 1971, 1973, 1975, 1977, 1995.

Printed in the United States of America

Typesetting by Andrew MacBride

Library of Congress Cataloging-in-Publication Data

Ruvolo, Carol J., 1946–
    Grace to stand firm, grace to grow : light from 1–2 Peter / Carol J. Ruvolo.
        p.   cm. — (Light for your path)
    Includes bibliographical references.
    ISBN-10: 0-87552-634-9 (pbk.)
    ISBN-13: 0-87552-634-8 (pbk.)
    1. Grace—Biblical teaching.   2. Bible. N.T. Peter—Study and teaching. I. Title.

BS2795.6.G73R88 2003
227'.9206—dc21

2002045048

For Marlene Hildabrand,
who persistently stands firm
and grows in the true grace of God

CONTENTS

Contents

ACKNOWLEDGMENTS

I want to express my deep gratitude for several dear saints whose support and encouragement made writing *Grace to Stand Firm, Grace to Grow* not only possible but also richly rewarding. Brendon and Joan O'Dowd read every chapter and blessed me with their rich insights into God's Word and the nature of fallen humanity. Without their contributions, the book would have been far more theoretical and far less useful. Daren Dietmeier, Ryan O'Dowd, and Barbara Ramey also read certain chapters and made suggestions that proved invaluable. I am forever indebted to each one of you.

John and Diana Hunt, Rob and Barbara Ramey, Blair Willis, Martin Ban, and Brendon and Joan helped me get through a few difficult months with generous amounts of love and wise counsel. Without them, *Grace to Stand Firm, Grace to Grow* would still be half finished with little hope of completion any time soon. Words fail to communicate how much I appreciate each one of you.

The ladies in the Tuesday afternoon discussion group patiently allowed me to contribute something I'd read, heard, or learned about Peter's epistles to almost very discussion. They served as iron sharpening iron as I struggled to understand and communicate Peter's perspective on Christian living. Thank you, dear friends, for helping me think.

Barbara Lerch at P&R Publishing was equally patient, typically wise, and characteristically loving as two or three deadlines went flying by with the book nowhere near completion. Thank you, dear Pooh, for your understanding and for your faithful reminders that I can only write it as fast as God gives it to me.

My family has, once again, been very supportive of the whole book-writing process, which, despite my best intentions, always seems to disrupt normal life (whatever that is!). I thank God for the many ways that each of you enrich and enliven my days on this earth.

And above all, I thank my Lord Jesus Christ for the grace that allows me to do what I do. I can think of no one as unqualified or unlikely as I to speak and write about God's revelation. But I also know that the more earthen the pot, the more glory He gets. So, my prayer is that this work of His grace will display His great glory!

Welcome to the Light for Your Path Series

The Light for Your Path Series is designed to help Christians learn how to glorify and enjoy God by living out their transformation in Jesus Christ. Each book in the series reflects the author's commitment to the Bible as the infallible, inerrant, authoritative, and entirely sufficient Word of God, and her conviction that Reformed theology is the clearest and most accurate restatement of biblical truth.

The series begins with two foundational studies centering on the Bible itself. *A Book Like No Other: What's So Special About the Bible* presents (in six lessons) the unique character of God's revelation. *Turning On the Light: Discovering the Riches of God's Word* provides (in seven lessons) an effective approach to studying the Bible. Combining these two books in a thirteen-week course will prepare new and veteran students to gain the most from the Light for Your Path Series.

The remaining studies in the series fall into two categories. "Light" studies cover particular *books* of the Bible (or sections of books, or groups of books such as the Gospels). These studies guide you through portions of Scripture, enabling you to understand and apply the meaning of each passage. You will recognize them by their subtitles, beginning with the words *Light from.*

"Focus" studies spotlight important *topics* in the Christian faith and life, such as prayer, salvation, righteousness, and relationships, and seek to show what the whole Bible says about them. These studies also stress understanding and applying biblical truth in daily life. Their subtitles begin with the words *Focus on.* Studying a combination of biblical books and topics will shed much-needed scriptural light on your walk with God. Both types of Bible study should be included in a "balanced diet" for a growing Christian.

The *Leader's Guide* that accompanies this series contains a complete description of the purpose and format of these studies, along with helpful suggestions for leading students through them.

Bible study is a serious task that involves a significant investment of time and energy. Preparing yourself to study effectively will help you reap the greatest benefit from that investment. Study when you are well rested and alert. Try to find a time and place that is quiet, free of distractions, and conducive to concentration. Use a loose-leaf or spiral notebook to take notes on what you read and to do the exercises in this study. You may also want to develop a simple filing system so that you can refer to these notes in later studies.

Approach Bible study as you would any task that requires thought and effort to do well. Don't be surprised if it challenges you and stretches your thinking. Expect it to be difficult at times but extremely rewarding.

Always begin your study with prayer. Ask the Lord to reveal sin in your life that needs to be confessed and cleansed, to help you concentrate on His truths, and to illumine your mind with understanding of what He has written. End your study with a prayer for opportunities to apply what you have learned and wisdom to recognize those opportunities when they occur.

Each lesson in these studies is followed by three types of exercises: Review, Application, and Digging Deeper. The review exercises will help you determine how well you understood the lesson material by giving you an opportunity to express the key points in your own words. The application exercises encourage you to put your understanding of the material to work in your daily life. And the digging deeper exercises challenge you to pursue further study in certain key areas.

You should be able to find the answers to the review questions in the lesson material, but please resist the temptation to copy words or phrases out of the lesson when you answer these questions. Work at putting these ideas into your own words. When you can do this, you know you have understood what you have read. It might help to ask yourself, "How would I explain this idea to someone else if I didn't have the book with me?"

If you don't have time to do all of the application exercises, pray over them and ask the Lord to show you which one(s) He wants you to work on. Because you will be applying the lessons to your daily life, these applications should take some time and thought. Answering one of them well will benefit you more than answering all of them superficially.

Answers to the application exercises should be very specific. Work at avoiding vague generalities. It might help to keep in mind that a specific application will provide specific answers to the questions Who? What? When? Where? and How? A vague generality will not. You can make applications in the areas of your thinking, your attitudes, and your behavior. (See lesson 6 of *Turning On the Light* for more about application.)

Digging deeper exercises usually require a significant amount of time and effort to complete. They were designed to provide a challenge for mature Christians who are eager for more advanced study. However, new Christians should not automatically pass them by. The Holy Spirit may choose to use one of them to help you grow. Remember that all

Christians grow by stretching beyond where they are right now. So if one or two of these exercises intrigue you, spend some time working on them. And do not hesitate to ask for help from your pastor, elders, teacher, or mature Christian friends.

As you work through this study, resist the temptation to compare yourself with other Christians in your group. The purpose of this study is to help you grow in your faith by learning and applying God's truth in your daily life—not to fill up a study book with brilliantly worded answers. If you learn and apply one element of God's truth in each lesson, you are consistently moving beyond where you were when you began.

Always remember that effective Bible study equips you to glorify God and enjoy Him forever. You glorify God when you live in such a way that those around you can look at you and see an accurate reflection of God's character and nature. You enjoy God when you are fully satisfied in His providential ordering of the circumstances in your life. When your life glorifies God and your joy is rooted in His providence, your impact on our fallen world will be tremendous.

Grace is the pleasure of God
to magnify the worth of God
by giving sinners the right and power
to delight in God
without obscuring the glory of God.
—*John Piper*

The Perspective

Cynthia Wilson resolutely stepped off the elevator into the short hallway of the bank's top floor. She took a deep breath and gazed at the oak door labeled Executive Suites. It wasn't the first time she'd been up here, but it was the first time she'd been up here when so much was at stake. She was being interviewed for a lateral promotion, a move up and across from the bank's operations department into the marketing area.

She had requested a position in marketing when she applied at Fidelity State Bank two years ago. Her degree was in marketing. She had finished top in her class. And she loved the field. But at the time she applied, there were no marketing positions available. Since jobs were scarce and she needed to work, she had accepted her current operations position with the HR consultant's assurance that she would be a front-runner for the first marketing opening.

This interview, however, wasn't for the first marketing opening. It was for the third. Twice now she had lost out to clearly less qualified people, and she had no idea why. The explanations in both cases had been tight-lipped and vague. But since jobs were still scarce and she still needed to work, she hadn't contested the seemingly unfair decisions. She had simply bided her time and applied again.

Oh, Lord, *Cynthia prayed.* Please help me make a good impression. You know how much this job means to me. I want to use the skills and abilities you helped me acquire. Please give me this job, and I'll work twice as hard to honor you in it. *She took another deep breath and tried not to look desperate as she opened the door.*

The executive secretary looked up and recognized her immediately. "Miss Wilson. It's good to see you again," *she said with the barest hint of a smile.* "Let me see if Mr. Bauer is ready to speak with you."

Five minutes later Cynthia was seated across from Mr. Bauer's enormous desk, listening to distressingly familiar words. "Miss Wilson, we appreciate your continuing interest in the marketing department and, as usual, your application is impressive. However, we have received several other impressive applications as well, and quite frankly, a few of those applicants appear to us to be better suited for this position. You're doing an excellent job where you are now, and we appreciate that. So please don't be discouraged. You know that marketing is a highly competitive field, and that we must consider a number of factors when filling positions."

Mr. Bauer started to rise, but Cynthia wanted to know why she was being routinely passed over. "Mr. Bauer," *she said.* "I would like to know what some of those factors are."

The man's jaw tightened, and he looked down at his desk. "Miss Wilson, we don't need to go into that. We are very happy with your work in operations."

"Well, I'm not," *Cynthia responded a little more boldly.* "I spent years preparing to work in marketing, and God has given me talent, ability, and a love for the field. Why do you believe I am not suited for it?"

"All right, if you must know. Your comment just now demonstrates why you are ill-suited for marketing. In a word, Miss Wilson, you are too blatantly Christian. You talk about God, Jesus Christ, and the Bible as if they have a bearing on every aspect of life. Fidelity State is a bank, Miss Wilson, not a church. We haven't said anything to you about the Bible

*you keep in plain sight on your desk, or about saying grace
in the cafeteria, or about the religious discussions you have
with other employees, because your work is excellent and
your colleagues haven't complained about your behavior.
However, marketing would require you to work closely with
prospective customers, advertisers, and respected, influen-
tial business and society people. We can't run the risk of you
offending them with your religion. Until you're more inclined
to keep your religion to yourself, you will not work in the
marketing department of this bank."*

*Too stunned to formulate a coherent response, Cynthia
mumbled a weak "Thank you, sir," and left the room with as
much dignity as she could muster. Anger and shame took
turns flooding her soul as she leaned against the back wall
of the elevator and wiped away tears.* Lord, I don't understand what's happening here. I'm trying hard to honor you
in my life. I never miss my daily devotions. I share my faith
whenever I can. I work at developing the fruit of the Spirit.
I'm not aware of any unconfessed sin. And yet you're withholding your blessing and not giving me the desire of my
heart. What am I doing wrong?

*When the elevator doors opened, Cynthia took one look at
the bustling lobby and hurried, head down, to her office to
regain her composure. She closed the door, sank into her
chair, and reached for a tissue. Then she heard a hesitant
knock followed by the soft voice of Abby, the department secretary.* "Miss Wilson, are you OK?"

"No," *Cynthia half sobbed and half laughed.* "Was it that
obvious?"

"Not really. I just happened to get a good look at your face
as you went by. May I come in?"

"Why not," *Cynthia sighed. Abby had worked at Fidelity
for many years, was active in a large Christian church across
town, and had a compassionate nature.* Maybe she can help
me think through this mess, *Cynthia mused.*

A few minutes and several tissues later, Abby had heard the whole story. "Miss Wilson," she said with a chuckle. "I think you're trying too hard."

"What?" Cynthia's face registered surprise and confusion. "Should I just give up on the idea of ever working in marketing?"

"No, no," Abby waved away Cynthia's comment. "You're not working too hard at your job. You're working too hard at your faith. You know you're saved by grace, right?"

"Of course," Cynthia nodded.

"Well, salvation by grace is a free gift from God. All we have to do is accept it. We're not under law; grace wiped that out. Once you've accepted God's free gift of salvation, you don't have to do good works to keep it. If you did, it wouldn't be free and it wouldn't be a gift. God won't take your salvation away, no matter what you do or don't do. That's one reason the gospel is called Good News. Another reason is that God loves you and wants you to have a good life.

"Miss Wilson," Abby continued, "God knows how much this job means to you, and He wants you to have it. He's not going to punish you if you put your Bible in the drawer and quit saying grace in the cafeteria in order to get a promotion. I hope you don't mind me being honest with you, but I think you're making your faith a lot harder than God intended it to be. And I think you're doing that because you don't really understand what it means to be saved by grace. Grace isn't about rules and regulations; it's about freedom. Once you're saved, you can pretty much do what you want."

Cynthia Wilson has just been blasted by one of the enemy's deadliest weapons—a spiritual shotgun, if you will, whose double barrel is labeled persecution and false doctrine. That spiritual shotgun is aimed at the biblical doctrine of grace. Satan takes aim at the doctrine of grace because it supports and strengthens our Christian walk through this world. Since he knows that we glorify God by walking worthy of our high calling in Christ (Eph. 4:1) and since he hates to see God get any glory, he develops weapons designed to reduce our worthy walk to an unworthy limp.[1]

Satan would like nothing better than to darken God's glory by stealing His children's salvation. But he knows he can't do that because God's grace surrounds them as an impregnable fortress. So he resorts to dimming God's glory by crippling our witness.

Satan knows that he doesn't have to damage the grace fortress in order to cripple our worthy walk. All he has to do is convince us that it's damaged. If he can undermine our assurance that we are saved, shake our confidence in God's empowering Spirit, or convince us that redemption entails no obedience, he can prevent us from giving God glory. So he picks up his trusty spiritual shotgun and aims persecution and false doctrine at our perception of grace. If either hits home, we're likely to stumble in our walk with the Lord. And if both find their mark, we may find ourselves face down in the dirt!

The blast Cynthia Wilson has just sustained could well knock her flat, because her understanding of grace was weak to begin with. She thought of grace only in terms of her initial salvation and didn't see its importance to living out that salvation. Cynthia's prayers reflect her belief that growing in Christ is entirely a matter of personal effort and that God's blessings depend on how hard she works. Her misperception of grace has made her a prime target for Satan's assault.

When persecution hit hard, her first response was to wonder, *What am I doing wrong?* That mindset weakened her defenses against a blast of false doctrine disguised as wise counsel. Her frustrated pursuit of blessing through effort may well incline her to think that Abby is right. Why work so hard only to reap persecution, when her mansion in glory is a free gift of God?

Is Cynthia's worthy walk about to disintegrate into an unworthy limp? Possibly, but not necessarily. She can repel Satan's assaults by reaching for that Bible she keeps in plain sight on her desk and using it to fortify her perception of grace. One of the best places to which she could turn would be the two short epistles written by Peter.

Peter wrote those letters to first-century Christians whose circumstances of life bore a close resemblance to Cynthia's, and also to ours. Most of them were being routinely harassed because they were Christians, and many were being harangued by glib teachers of heresy. You see, Satan's spiritual shotgun is not a new weapon. He's been blasting away at the worthy walk of believers down through the centuries. And when he succeeds in dimming God's glory by damaging a believer's perception of grace, he jumps for joy.

Peter knew that believers scattered throughout the region we know as Turkey were under attack. And he knew what they needed to stand firm in defense of the glory of God. Peter, just like Jesus' brother James, was a practical theologian. He didn't send these beleaguered believers a tightly reasoned theological treatise. Instead, he sent them a user's manual. He knew that the last thing they needed was a doctrine of suffering. They weren't sitting around speculating about why bad things happen to godly people. They were under attack and needed some weapons.

Peter, who had been under attack a few times himself, gave them the tried and true weapons that had worked best for him: hope and encouragement. But he didn't hold out a whimsical pie-in-the-sky kind of hope or offer an ethereal "let's win one for the Gipper" type of encouragement. Rather, he effectively armed them for battle by anchoring their hope in the true grace of God and bolstering their courage with firm exhortations to grow in that grace. He told them that their worthy walk would not disintegrate into an unworthy limp if they understood and applied God's revealed truth about grace.

If they recalled to mind that the same grace that saved them would also sustain them, and if they faithfully lived out that knowledge in difficult circumstances, they would fulfill their high calling to glorify God. If they pursued deeper knowledge of the grace that appeared in the Lord Jesus Christ and if they obeyed out of love instead of selfish desire, they would not be carried away by the error of unprincipled men or fall from their own steadfastness. In short, if they fortified their perception of grace, they would not succumb to the double-barreled assault of persecution and false doctrine.

Peter's perspective of grace helped our first-century brothers and sisters live out their high calling in Christ even in the midst of satanic attack. And it speaks just as clearly to us twenty-one centuries later. Paul warned his protégé Timothy that "all who desire to live godly in Christ Jesus will be persecuted" (2 Timothy 3:12), and Peter admonished his readers not to be surprised at the "fiery ordeal" among them (1 Peter 4:12). Bible commentator and historian J. N. D. Kelly was speaking biblical truth when he said that persecution, with the temptation to apostasy, is the atmosphere in which Christians live.[2]

Satan does indeed prowl about like a roaring lion, seeking someone to devour. And those whose lives are reflecting God's glory best are his first choice on the menu. If we want to walk worthy of our high calling in Christ, we need to listen to Peter and apply what he says. We need to stand firm and grow in the true grace of God.

Notes

1. My references here to Satan's assaults against Christians should be understood in the broadest possible sense. Since Satan is a created being who cannot be in more than one place at a time, he is not involved personally in every assault on believers. Temptations to sin and thereby to obscure God's glory come from three sources: the world, the flesh, and the devil. However, since Satan, out of hatred for God, instigated the fall, we can speak of assaults from the world and the flesh as coming from him in an ultimate sense. David Powlison in *Power Encounters* describes the "three stranded braid" we must deal with: "Our social situation feeds us a stream of beguilements and threats; our own hearts gravitate to lies and lusts; the devil schemes to aggravate sin and unbelief. . . . The world, the flesh, and the devil work in concert. The Bible differentiates the three strands . . . without dividing them. The Bible never teaches that we have three sorts of problems: one set termed world problems, a second set identified as flesh problems, and a third set called 'spiritual' problems" (*Power Encounters: Reclaiming Spiritual Warfare* [Grand Rapids: Baker, 1995], 109).

2. J. N. D. Kelly, *Black's New Testament Commentaries: The Epistles of Peter and Jude,* ed. Henry Chadwick (London: A&C Black, 1969; Peabody, Mass.: Hendrickson, 1969), 9.

1

Grace to Stand Firm

The grace of God in the heart of man is a tender plant in a strange, unkindly soil. Therefore, it cannot grow unless great care is taken by a skillful hand that cherishes it. To this end, God has given the constant ministry of the Word to his church, not only for the first work of conversion, but also for increasing his grace in the hearts of his children. —Robert Leighton

Primary Passage
1 Peter 1:1–5

Supplementary Passages
Exodus 24:1–11
Proverbs 4:11–19
John 3:1–21
Acts 2:22–24
Romans 6:4–7; 8:28–39
Ephesians 1:3–14
Philippians 3:7–16
Colossians 1:3–8
2 Thessalonians 2:13–15
2 Timothy 1:12
Hebrews 9:18–28; 12:18–29

Before reading the lesson material, please read the primary Scripture passage listed above and as many of the supplementary passages as time allows. Then briefly summarize in your notebook what you have read. (Do not go into detail. Limit your summary to a brief description of the people, events, and/or ideas discussed in the passages.)

1

The Hope
of Salvation

Sanctification is justification in action.

—Jerry Dodson

Writing shortly before his death in June of 2000, James Montgomery Boice expressed grave concern over the evangelical church's rampant desertion of the great biblical doctrines reaffirmed by the Reformation. The church's wholesale abandonment of the five "solas" (*sola Scriptura, solus Christus, sola gratia, sola fide,* and *soli Deo gloria*), Boice concluded, is largely due to the fact that Christians "have forgotten God and are not really living for his glory."[1]

Boice's *Whatever Happened to the Gospel of Grace?* is his definitive word on a subject that was dear to his heart—the witness of Christians to God's glorious grace. In it he describes how the church's once powerful testimony has decisively weakened as we have embraced "the world's wisdom, the world's theology, the world's agenda, and the world's methods."[2] This weakening of our witness is a serious problem because we were created and saved to show forth God's glory as we live out His gospel of grace in every situation of life.

His words struck a strong cord with me. The heart and soul of my ministry is urging, exhorting, and encouraging Christians to walk worthy of their high calling in Christ. As I minister among family and friends here in Albuquerque and travel the country speaking at retreats and conferences, I encounter a distressingly high number of Christians who *can't define* what their high calling is. Even more distressing is the number of Christians who *know* their high calling is displaying God's glory but who don't have a clue about *how* to do it. One Air Force chaplain, who has an extensive biblical counseling ministry, recently told me, "This whole glorifying God thing is rocket science to most Christians."

We need help getting back on track. And James Boice's book is a good place to start. In it he calls believers to repent, recover, and renew. He urges the church to repent of its worldliness, to recover again the biblical doctrines that were once (but sadly not for all) recovered by the Reformers, and to renew our witness by living lives truly transformed by the gospel of grace.

He asks, "Can we have that power again in our day?" and answers, "We can. But only if we hold to the full-orbed Reformation gospel and do not compromise with the culture around us." He then asks, "How does it happen?" And he answers, "It happens by renewing our minds, . . . by study of the life-giving and renewing Word of God . . . empowered by the Holy Spirit [so that] we will begin to take on something of the glorious luster of the Lord Jesus Christ and will become increasingly like him."[3]

Boice obviously thought that the doctrines reaffirmed five hundred years ago by men known as the Reformers were very special—and he was right. They were very special, not because of the men who affirmed them but because they were and still are biblical truth. At that time in history, their recovery called the church to repent and renew by resetting its focus on its sovereign God. When God's people heeded that call, their revitalized witness launched a revival of mammoth proportions. The world saw God's power displayed in the lives of weak saints and heard His truth proclaimed in the words of saved sinners. As God's people recovered and applied biblical truth about grace, they returned to walking worthy of their high calling in Christ.

Boice assures us that the same thing will happen at our time in history if we will repent of our worldliness, recover the biblical truths about grace, and renew our commitment to living them out. He concluded *Whatever Happened to the Gospel of Grace?* with this exhortation: "Genuine religion does make a difference in one's life, which is precisely what we need. . . . So let's get on with our calling, and let those who say they know God show they actually do—for his glory and for the good of all."[4]

James Montgomery Boice was not the first godly leader to encourage God's people to live in and live out the powerful principles of God's sovereign grace. Neither were the Reformers. Long before any of them put pen to paper (or fingers to keyboard), Peter, an apostle of Jesus Christ, exhorted first-century Christians to stand firm and grow in the true grace of God.

Peter's Perspective on Christian Living

One of the things I find most endearing about Peter is that he had been truly transformed by the gospel of grace. The apostle who wrote the epistles we're studying had come a long way since his brother Andrew introduced him to Jesus. On that day he was Simon, a self-reliant, self-confident, first-century fisherman—so sure of himself that he appeared cocky and arrogant. My guess is that Simon had little, if any, understanding of grace on the day he met Jesus. If he had been asked to define it, he might have scratched his head and looked puzzled. Grace would have been hard for him to define because he hadn't experienced it.

But that would soon change. Jesus had come into the world to introduce Simon and all the rest of God's chosen children to God's gospel of grace. Shortly after they met, Jesus called Simon out of the world to be redeemed by God's grace. Then He sent him back into the world to live by God's grace. By God's grace, He transformed Simon, a self-focused fisher of fish, into Peter, a God-focused fisher of men. And by God's grace, He molded him into the man God had chosen from before time began to lead His new covenant church.

By the time Peter sat down to write his first epistle to beleaguered believers scattered throughout Pontus, Galatia, Cappadocia, Asia, and Bithynia, he could give them much more than a definition of grace. He could give them a description of how Christian living takes place within the context of grace.

Peter had learned that those who trust in God's grace for their redemption must also rely on His grace for their sanctification. He knew that believers have no strength in themselves to walk worthy of their high calling in Christ. He knew that believers cannot fulfill their chief end by human effort alone. He knew that working out our salvation depends upon God's working in us to accomplish His purposes.

Peter knew that power for Christian living is as gracious a gift as is salvation. We don't deserve it or earn it any more than we do our redemption. Peter would have agreed with Jerry Bridges, who emphasized that grace, which he defined as "God's free and unmerited favor shown to guilty sinners who deserve only judgment,"[5] has two dimensions. God's free and unmerited favor is first extended to us in our salvation when we are forgiven and accepted in Christ. Then grace is further extended to us in our sanctification as we are delivered from the dominion of sin and filled with the enabling power of the Holy Spirit through our union with Christ.[6]

Peter's understanding of grace hadn't come easily. His self-sufficiency had proved a hard nut to crack. But crack it, God did. He simply allowed Peter to lean on himself until he fell hard enough to squash his pride flat. Like so many of us, Peter had to experience the futility of self-reliance before he learned to lean on God's power instead. Watching him grow in grace through the biblical accounts of his life is very encouraging![7]

Reading his epistles is also encouraging, because they reflect the maturity he had attained by God's grace. The man who penned these two letters had learned to stand firm and grow in the true grace of God. He knew that his salvation and his sanctification were works of God's grace. He knew that he couldn't walk worthy of his high calling in Christ without God's gracious enabling any more than he could have earned his redemption. Peter's knowledge of what God had done for him, in him, and through him forged a distinctive perspective of Christian living—one that was grace-conscious, grace-filled, and grace-dependent.

It is this distinctive perspective of Christian living that he shares with first-century Christians who were being blasted by Satan's double-barreled assault of persecution and false doctrine.

Peter's Perspective Is Rooted in the Reality of Salvation
(1 Peter 1:1–2)

The folks to whom Peter wrote his first epistle were being assaulted by persecution. Most commentators believe that the persecution they were enduring had not yet escalated into official, state-sponsored oppression. Instead, it probably took the form of social ostracism, neighborly hostility, and pressure from authority figures such as husbands and slave owners.[8] Although they were most likely not yet suffering intensely, they were definitely uncomfortable in their surroundings. Their situation bears a close resemblance to what most of us reading this book may be enduring. I have yet to suffer intense "official," state-sponsored persecution because I am a Christian. But I have been slighted, snubbed, ridiculed, and "pressured" because of my faith. If you're working hard to live out your faith, I'm sure you have been too.

Peter wrote to encourage those first-century Christians to stand firm in God's grace. He may have sensed that the battle had just begun and that these opening skirmishes could serve well as strength-building exercises. Perhaps he saw in their situation a good opportunity for training them in the use of their spiritual weaponry. He knew that God gives believers everything they need in their faith to defend against every kind of assault, and that effectively standing against persecution provides a marvelous testimony of God's glorious grace. So Peter wrote a practical handbook on spiritual warfare telling his readers how to glorify God while enduring harsh treatment.

He began by reminding them of the way God had saved them. They had been "chosen according to the foreknowledge of God the Father, by the sanctifying work of the Spirit, to obey Jesus Christ and be sprinkled with His blood" (1:1–2). Their salvation had come solely through the work of their trinitarian God (God the Father, God the Son, and God the Holy Spirit), not through their efforts.

God the Father had chosen them according to His foreknowledge, which Peter's first recorded sermon in Acts indicates was much more than His awareness of future events.

In Acts 2:23, Peter told the Pentecost crowd that "this Man [Jesus], delivered over by the predetermined plan and foreknowledge of God, you nailed to a cross by the hands of godless men and put Him to death." Certainly God did not look down the corridors of time, see that in the first century A.D. godless men would kill Jesus Christ, and plan redemption accordingly. Scripture is clear that redemption was planned before time began and was worked out in history by God's sovereign providence (Ephesians 1:3–14; 2 Thessalonians 2:13–14; Titus 1:1–3).

God the Holy Spirit had sanctified them or set them apart for God's purposes of redemption. He had called them out of the world of lost sinners by doing three things: convicting them concerning sin, righteousness, and judgment (John 16:8–11); illumining their minds to understand God's truth (1 Corinthians 2:6–16); and giving them the new life that seeks God's kingdom and righteousness (John 6:63–65).

God the Son shed His blood on the cross, making full atonement for their sin and propitiating[9] God's just wrath against them so that they could be cleansed, forgiven, and adopted into His family (Romans 3:21–26). The work of all three members of the Trinity had brought Peter's readers into a relationship of obedience to Jesus Christ.

Peter's mention of their being sprinkled with Christ's blood is most likely a reference to the children of Israel being sprinkled with the blood of the covenant when they promised to obey all that the Lord had spoken to them through Moses (Exodus 24:1–8).[10] The children of Israel proceeded to fail miserably in keeping that promise, but Peter had higher hopes for his new covenant brethren. Pentecost had given them the fullest measure of God's indwelling Spirit. They had the very power of God living within them. All the resources they needed to glorify God in the midst of difficult circumstances had been given to them in the grace of salvation.

Peter addressed them as aliens saved by God's grace, those who had been called out of the world for the purpose of redemption and sent back into the world for the purpose of testimony. They were no longer of the world but were in the world to bear witness of God's glory. And to do that effectively, they needed His grace and peace in fullest measure.

Grace would equip them to rely on God's strength to stand firm, and peace (the internal contentment resulting from trusting God) would reflect God's power to those around them. I have a hunch that Peter's greeting, "May grace and peace be yours in fullest measure" (1:2), was also a prayer asking God to equip these believers to glorify Him in their difficult circumstances.

Peter's Perspective Is Lived Out in Living Hope
(1 Peter 1:3–5)

Edmund Clowney captured a sparkling facet of Peter's perspective on Christian living when he said that Christians are transients in this world, but they are not wanderers.[11] Christians are indeed passing through without settling down in this world, but they're passing through with a clear purpose and destination in mind.

Christians in the world know why they are here and where they are going. They know that God's grace redeemed them out of the world's sinful system, freed them from sin's enslavement, and guaranteed them eternal life in the mansions of heaven. They know that they no longer live for themselves but for the Lord. They know that God "according to His great mercy has caused [them] to be born again to a living hope through the resurrection of Jesus Christ" (1:3).

A living hope is one that does more than hang on for

dear life and think optimistically. A living hope is one that energizes righteous activity and exudes godly enthusiasm because it is grounded in God-centered reality. It rests in the fact of Christ's resurrection, stimulates a walk that is worthy of the highest of callings, and anticipates an inheritance that is imperishable, undefiled, and unfading. Clowney describes it as a sure hope that holds the future in the present because it is anchored in the past.[12]

God acted mercifully to satisfy His wrath against the sin of those He had chosen when He sent Jesus Christ to die on the cross. When He raised Jesus from the dead, He accepted His atoning sacrifice for our sins. Since the requirements of His holy justice had been fully served, He declared us righteous in Christ and adopted us into His family. As His chosen children, we came into an inheritance that is reserved for us in heaven. Our inheritance is secure in its perfect environment because there it cannot be destroyed, harmed, or diminished in value. It will be there, in all its glory, when we arrive.

And God also assures us that we will arrive. When Jesus Christ rose from the dead, He ascended to the right hand of the Father. There He continually intercedes for us, guaranteeing that nothing in all of creation can ever separate us from the love of God (Romans 8:35–39). Our living hope is firmly anchored in Christ's resurrection, which not only secures our inheritance but also attests that God will protect us in this world until we are glorified in the next (John 17:14–17; Romans 8:30; 1 Peter 1:5).

The living hope of salvation energized the first-century Christians to whom Peter wrote to stand firm in God's grace in the face of persecution. It kept them from forgetting God and not really living for His glory. As we read on in Peter's epistle, we'll see how it did that. Will you take a few moments before going on to the exercises to thank God for His gospel of grace and for the living hope that it brings you? Will you then ask Him to teach you, through Peter's letter, how to stand firm in that grace in all circumstances of life so that you will live for His glory?

Notes

1. James Montgomery Boice, *Whatever Happened to the Gospel of Grace? Recovering the Doctrines That Shook the World* (Wheaton, Ill.: Crossway, 2001), 36.

2. Ibid., 21–23.

3. Material in this paragraph was taken from Lane T. Dennis's publisher's foreword to *Whatever Happened to the Gospel of Grace?*

4. Boice, *Gospel of Grace,* 210.

5. Jerry Bridges, *Transforming Grace: Living Confidently in God's Unfailing Love* (Colorado Springs: NavPress, 1991), 21.

6. Jerry Bridges, *The Discipline of Grace: God's Role and Our Role in the Pursuit of Holiness* (Colorado Springs: NavPress, 1994), 89.

7. See Carol J. Ruvolo, *Footprints of the Fisherman: Life Lessons from One Who Walked Closely with Christ* (Los Alamos, N.M.: Deo Volente Publishing, 2001), to trace Peter's growth in grace through the biblical accounts of his life.

8. Official state-sponsored oppression under cruel Roman emperors was not far off, but since Peter makes no mention of it in his letter, many commentators believe he wrote before it began.

9. *Propitiation* is a wonderful word that all Christians should understand and use. It refers to Christ's satisfaction of God's wrath against the sin of the elect that fulfilled the demands of God's holy justice so that we could be adopted into His family.

10. Wayne Grudem's insights into this passage are thought provoking and intriguing. If you have the time and the inclination, read pages 52–54 of his Tyndale New Testament commentary, *1 Peter* (Grand Rapids: Eerdmans, 1988).

11. Edmund Clowney, *The Bible Speaks Today: The Message of 1 Peter,* ed. John R. W. Stott (Downers Grove, Ill.: InterVarsity Press, 1988), 41.

12. Ibid., 44.

Exercises

Review

1. Describe James Montgomery Boice's grave concern about the evangelical church expressed in *Whatever Happened to the Gospel of Grace?* Explain the seriousness of his concern and briefly summarize what should be done to remedy the situation.

2. Briefly describe Peter's perspective on Christian living. How did he acquire this perspective?

3. Define *grace* and explain its two dimensions. Then explain the significance of both dimensions to Christian living.

4. What do you think were Peter's reasons for beginning his letter to persecuted Christians with a descriptive reminder of how they had been saved?

5. Support (using Scripture) the statement, "The phrase *according to His foreknowledge* refers to much more than God's awareness of future events."

6. According to 1 Peter 1:1–2, for what purpose are Christians saved? What role does grace play in fulfilling that purpose?

7. Discuss Edmund Clowney's description of a living hope as one that "holds the future in the present because it is anchored in the past."

8. Describe your inheritance as a Christian. How do you know you will receive it?

Application

1. This week begin memorizing one or more of the following Scripture passages:

   Romans 8:35–39
   2 Thessalonians 2:13–15
   2 Timothy 1:12

2. This week use Ephesians 1:3–14; Philippians 3:7–16; Romans 6:1–18; and Romans 8:1–39 to help you pray for a deeper understanding of God's grace in your life and for the boldness to live in and live out the gospel of grace.

3. Many Bible teachers say that the definition of a Christian is found in 1 Peter 1:1–2. A Christian, they say, is

one who is "chosen according to the foreknowledge of God the Father, by the sanctifying work of the Spirit, to obey Jesus Christ and be sprinkled with His blood." Identify the four defining characteristics of a Christian contained in these verses, and then explain the essential role of each in defining a Christian. (Reading the supplemental Scripture passages listed at the beginning of this lesson will help you.) Do you think this is a complete definition of a Christian? Explain. Apply the definition to yourself. Does it give you assurance that you are saved? If so, thank God in prayer for His graciousness to you. If not, talk to your pastor, a leader of your church, or a close Christian friend or relative who can help you examine yourself to see if you are in the faith.

4. Are you experiencing any difficulties or trials at this time in your life? If so, briefly describe them. Then describe how the living hope of salvation encourages you in the midst of them.

Digging Deeper

1. Based on what you have learned in this lesson and other research you may want to do, defend Jerry Dodson's statement, "Sanctification is justification in action."

2. Read *Whatever Happened to the Gospel of Grace?* Then use what you learn to develop a discipling tool you can use to help other Christians remember God and live for His glory.

Primary Passage
1 Peter 1:6–12

Supplementary Passages
Genesis 22:1–19
Psalms 30:5; 56
Daniel 12:3
Habakkuk 3:17–19
Matthew 5:10–16
Luke 24:13–27
John 20:24–29
Romans 5:3–5; 8:14–18
1 Corinthians 2:12–16; 4:5; 15:3–5
2 Corinthians 4:16–18; 5:7
Hebrews 12
James 1:2–8
1 John 4:7–21

Before reading the lesson material, please read the primary Scripture passage listed above and as many of the supplementary passages as time allows. Then briefly summarize in your notebook what you have read. (Do not go into detail. Limit your summary to a brief description of the people, events, and/or ideas discussed in the passages.)

2

The Joy of
Divine Testing

*For Peter, the reason the Christians were suffering was
because they had the results of salvation in their lives,
and their Christian living was now grating against a
sinful society. . . . Suffering, when properly understood
and applied, is the wake following behind salvation's
boat.* —Scot McKnight

A few years ago, a friend asked me whether I thought persecution was a good indicator of an effective witness. My
first reaction was to say "Absolutely!" But then I thought,
*Wait a minute . . . persecution may also reflect an obnoxious
witness.* So I told my friend that before we assume that
we're suffering for righteousness sake, we need to make
sure it's the gospel and not our behavior that's offensive
to others.

Scripture affirms that suffering in the form of persecution is a natural result of Christian living (2 Timothy 3:12;
1 Peter 4:12). But it also exhorts us to do our best to live in
peace with all men (Romans 12:18) and to behave in ways

that give unbelievers no genuine grounds for their slander (1 Peter 2:12; 3:15–16). Living distinctively Christian enough to draw persecution solely for righteousness sake isn't easy. Most of us do it poorly at best.

We tend to drift toward one extreme or the other. Some of us can get downright rude, or at least insensitive and inconsiderate, in the name of evangelism or discipling or exhortation, whereas others of us are so "at peace with all men" that we aren't distinctively Christian. In our day, it seems that more of us lean toward the second extreme than toward the first. My guess is that very few of us who read Scot McKnight's words introducing this lesson could illustrate them with examples from our experience!

Twenty-first-century American Christians, in general, are not suffering for having "the results of salvation in their lives." Their lifestyles don't "grate against a sinful society." The "wake" behind their salvation hardly stirs up a ripple, much less any waves.[1] Why is it that salvation in our day and culture doesn't draw persecution the way it did when Peter wrote this epistle? Is it because our society is less sinful, and thus less antagonistic, toward Christianity now? Or is it because the way Christians live no longer raises society's hackles?

Scot McKnight addresses those questions in his commentary on 1 Peter:

> Our *lack* of suffering is, in part, due to a *lack of nerve* on the part of the church to challenge our contemporary world with the message of the cross and to live according to the teachings of Jesus with uncompromising vigor. . . . As a guiding [biblical] principle, then, those who live faithful lives in an unbelieving world will find opposition to both their ideas and their practices. . . . The contrast between the Christian community's belief in the gospel as

well as its commitment to holy living and our culture's unbelief in the gospel and its permissiveness *ought to generate more sparks* than it does. I contend that one of the reasons there are so few sparks is because the fires of commitment and unswerving confession of the truth of the gospel are too frequently set on low flame, as if the church grows best if it only simmers rather than boils.[2]

Ouch! Do his words convict you as keenly as they do me? Genuine Christianity lived out in sinful society (and our society qualifies) grates severely enough to generate sparks. Those sparks represent the antagonism that's been promised to those who "desire to live godly in Christ Jesus" (2 Timothy 3:12). When sparks are routinely and consistently absent, we're not doing our jobs.

The message of 1 Peter is one of hope and encouragement for Christians who are doing their jobs. It tells us to stand firm in God's grace when the sparks start to fly. But it assumes that the sparks are indeed flying—because our witness is boiling, not set on simmer.

Are you part of the group to whom Peter is speaking? Are you generating a few sparks because your Christian witness is boiling? Are some of those sparks landing on you and burning a bit? If so, read on and be greatly encouraged. If not, please stop at this point, as I have done, and evaluate how at peace you are with the world. Do you need to repent of your worldliness, recover God's truths, and renew your commitment to living them out? I certainly did. If you need to also, please do it now before you read on.

Why Be a Christian If You Get Persecution?
Paul tells us that people in their "natural" (unsaved) state cannot "accept the things of the Spirit of God" because they

appear foolish to them (1 Corinthians 2:14). The promise of persecution for Christians surely falls in that category! Why would anyone cast their lot with a Savior who assures them that following Him faithfully will cause them to suffer? Peter's answer to that very reasonable question is simple enough: Christians accept persecution, and even rejoice in their suffering, because that's not all they've been promised.

Christians have also been promised an inheritance that is imperishable, undefiled, and will not fade away. They have also been promised protection by the power of God, which assures them that nothing can separate them from His love. And they have also been assured that God keeps His promises. Pie-crust promises perhaps? Easily made, easily broken? Not on your life. God's divine promises were not easily made, because they required the death of His Son. And they cannot be easily broken, because a god who breaks promises is not God.

But simply knowing God's promises doesn't mean that we'll trust them. Until our fallen souls are regenerated and we are given Christ's mind (1 Corinthians 2:16), God's promises appear foolish to us. Until His Holy Spirit moves into our hearts and bears witness with our spirits that we are children of God, we will not understand that "the sufferings of this present time are not worthy to be compared with the glory that is to be revealed to us" (Romans 8:15–18).

Trusting God to keep His promises is what we call faith. We receive faith as a gift from God when we are regenerated (Ephesians 2:8–9; 2 Peter 1:1). We use the faith we've been given to trust in Christ for our salvation and to trust in God for the power to live for His glory. Faith is not our contribution to our salvation, because we have no faith to contribute until God gives it to us when He regenerates us. Nor is faith believing fervently enough to make things happen, because faith is not magic. God makes things happen; we don't.

The author of Hebrews defines faith as assurance and conviction that God is trustworthy and our hope in Him is true. Faith is the great motivator that fuels our worthy walk through this world—especially when our grating witness throws off some sparks. It sets our minds on the things above. It fixes our sights on the joy set before us instead of the trials all around us. It equips us to rejoice in all circumstances, to believe in and love a Savior we've never seen, and to bet our lives on the fulfillment of God's gracious promises. Faith is the most valuable thing Christians possess because it equips us to fulfill the chief end of our lives--to glorify God and enjoy Him forever.

The Sure Triumph of Faith
(1 Peter 1:6–9)

The Christians to whom Peter wrote his first epistle were unusual folks. I say that because they were rejoicing in the midst of various trials. And that's an unusual response to difficult circumstances! Most of the Christians I know (myself included) aren't inclined to rejoice in the midst of various trials. We're more likely to get angry, quake in fear, dissolve in self-pity, or question God's love. Even if we manage to keep an eternal perspective and set our sights on God's promises, we tend to look at hard times as occasions for teeth-gritting endurance instead of rejoicing.

Most commentators agree that Peter was not commanding these folks to rejoice in the midst of their various trials, although the Greek word he used could be translated that way. The context indicates that he was more likely commending them for their attitude toward difficult circumstances before he moved on to a discussion of holy behavior.[3] Peter knew that right attitudes underlying godly behavior glorify God in spectacular ways. And he knew that right attitudes are harder to come by than is right behavior. Therefore, he encouraged these suffering saints to maintain their godly outlook on life.

Peter bolstered their joy with a timely reminder that earthly trials are temporary and necessary. In the light of eternity, they can indeed be perceived as "momentary, light affliction" (2 Corinthians 4:17). And in the light of God's sovereignty, they can be received as integral elements in the outworking of God's ultimate purpose. John Calvin said that Peter's "purpose was to show that God does not thus try His people without reason, for if God afflicted us without cause, it would be grievous to bear."[4]

My good friend, D. J., knows these truths well and lives them out even better. When her daughter Sarah was killed by a drunk driver going the wrong way on an Arizona highway, D. J. was quite naturally thrown into a maelstrom of grief. But those of us who quickly rushed to her side were encouraged to see that the depth of her faith exceeded even the great depth of her grief. We saw her rejoice in the midst of her trial—not because her beloved daughter's life had been senselessly ended, but because she understood God's purpose for trials. D. J. knew that her trial was both necessary and temporary. She knew that God loved her (and her family, and Sarah) too much to allow them to suffer without a good reason. And she knew that this trial, like all others, would one day dissolve in the blaze of God's glory. Her faith in the truth equipped her to rejoice in the midst of her suffering.

In much the same way, Peter's readers rejoiced in the midst of their trials. They had their hearts, minds, and souls set on the end result of their trials instead of the present distress of those trials. They were running their race with endurance and without losing heart because they were imitating the example of Jesus, who "for the joy set before Him endured the cross, despising the shame, and has sat down at the right hand of the throne of God" (Hebrews 12:1–3).

By no stretch of the imagination could we say that Jesus enjoyed the cross. But we can safely say that He rejoiced in its purpose. Christ agonized in Gethsemane over His coming ordeal; He was not looking forward to being forsaken by God. However, He knew that the temporary affliction He would endure was required for the salvation of God's elect. Looking beyond the affliction to its end result equipped Jesus to suffer with an attitude of rejoicing.

Peter knew that the similar attitude of the Christians to whom he was writing sprang from their faith in Christ Jesus. He told them that their faith was more precious than gold, which although the most precious of metals, would eventually perish. Their faith, by contrast, was a gift of God and thus indestructible.

Their faith had come to them from God in absolute purity, only to be alloyed upon their receipt of it with their fallen sinfulness. Although precious and durable, it was in need of the refinement provided by testing. Their fallen bent toward unbelief obscured faith's perfection. Trials brought opportunities to watch God at work and trust His promises. Growing trust in God's Word eroded their doubts and refined more and more unbelief out of their faith. They could rejoice in trials because the pure faith God had given them was being revealed with increasing clarity to the praise of His glory.

God's grace working in them and through them equipped them to exercise faith and see it increasingly purified. This process revealed the presence of God's Spirit within them and bore incontrovertible witness to their transformation in Christ. It filled them with confidence that they were indeed children of God and would surely receive their inheritance. In the words of Edmund Clowney, they were living "in a future that is already present, not just in imagination or expectation, but in realization: the reality of Christ's presence in the Spirit."[5]

As the faith of these Christians was being "tested by fire" (1 Peter 1:7) and becoming increasingly pure, two glorious things were happening to them. First, they were becoming increasingly eager to see their Savior. The more they relied on His Spirit to help them walk worthy of their high calling in Christ, the more they longed to see Jesus revealed in praise, glory, and honor. And the more they also longed to hear Him bestow praise, glory, and honor on them when He said, "Well done, good and faithful servants."

Second, their love and belief in Christ was growing stronger and being reflected in their faithful attitude. Their love was evidenced in their desire to promote His glory, to delight in doing His will, and to spend eternity with Him. Their belief in Him was clearly demonstrated by their confident trust in the sufficiency of His work of salvation. The fact that they had never seen Jesus in person underscored the genuineness of their faith, and the genuineness of their faith assured them of their reward. As Augustine said, "It is the proper work of faith to believe what you do not see, and the reward of faith to see what you have believed."[6]

These unusual Christians were rejoicing in the midst of various trials because their faith had a "forward-looking and other worldly dimension"[7] that is often lacking among American Christians today. I see it in a few folks, like my friend D. J., but I don't see it often. We have a lot to learn from the example of our first-century brethren. Their worthy walk through this world was no unworthy limp. Their testimony was grating on their culture and generating some sparks. But they were rejoicing—with joy inexpressible and full of glory. Their unusual attitude came from their eternal perspective. They were looking beyond momentary affliction to the joy set before them—the sure result of the full, final, complete, and glorious salvation of their souls.

Excel Still More!
(1 Peter 1:10–12)

Peter must have been thrilled with their unusual attitude because he was almost effusive in encouraging them to maintain it. He didn't stop with commending them for it and reminding them of how important it was to stick to it. He went on to proclaim how blessed they were to be born and reborn on this side of the cross. Although their culture considered them insignificant and worthy of scorn, they understood truth that had puzzled the prophets and played key roles in a drama that still captivates angels.

Peter's words in this passage seem intended to raise their already commendable walk through this world to new heights of worthiness. Although delighted with their current practice, he urges them to excel even more. They did well to rejoice in various trials because of their assurance that the trials were temporary, necessary, and "light" in comparison with the eternal weight of future glory. However, they would do better to expand their rejoicing with an infusion of gratitude for their salvation in Christ.

The Christians to whom Peter was writing were among the first to be blessed with a panoramic view of redemption. They were among the first to understand that the words of the prophets, which the prophets didn't understand fully, had been fulfilled in the gospel that Peter's readers had heard and believed. They were among the first to stand awestruck in the face of complete revelation.

They, of all people, had grounds for rejoicing in what God had accomplished. They, of all people, had reason to be grateful for the gift of salvation. They, of all people, could excel still more by enhancing their joy with the glory of gratitude. We, who have had twenty-one centuries to ponder the wonder of God's plan of redemption, have even more reason to rejoice and give thanks. We, of all people, should exceed their excelling.

But too often we don't. Decades of familiarity with full revelation seem to have dulled that initial sense of amazement. We're so accustomed to living on this side of the cross that we no longer see it for the great blessing it is. Our worship, our witness, and our walk languish because we've ceased to be stunned by what God has done. We're downright blasé (dare I say bored) with the old gospel story that caused the prophets to wonder and still fascinates angels.

Before we move on to consider Peter's discussion of holy behavior, we need to focus on adjusting our attitudes. As you work through the exercises that follow, consider your outlook on Christian living in light of the way Peter's first readers lived. Are you rejoicing in the midst of various trials? Is your faith being tested and strengthened as you face adversity? Are you looking forward to the praise, glory, and honor to come? Is your love for and belief in Christ growing daily? Does "joy inexpressible and full of glory" (1:8) characterize your outlook on life? Are you simply stunned by the blessing of being born and reborn on this side of the cross?

Notes

1. I want to reaffirm that my remarks in this paragraph are addressed to most Christians living in the United States of America. I am intensely aware of the grievous fact that many of our brothers and sisters in other parts of the world are suffering greatly because of their faithful witness to the gospel of Jesus Christ. Their example is convicting to those of us who are rarely called to risk much of anything in kingdom service.

2. Scot McKnight, *The NIV Application Commentary: 1 Peter* (Grand Rapids: Zondervan, 1996), 74–75, his italics.

3. For a representative view, see J. N. D. Kelly, *Black's New Testament Commentaries: The Epistles of Peter and Jude,* ed. Henry Chadwick (London: A&C Black, 1969; Peabody, Mass.: Hendrickson, 1969), 53.

4. Quoted in Wayne Grudem, *The Tyndale New Testament Commentaries: 1 Peter* (Grand Rapids: Eerdmans, 1988), 62.

5. Edmund Clowney, *The Bible Speaks Today: The Message of 1 Peter,* ed. John R. W. Stott (Downers Grove, Ill.: InterVarsity Press, 1988), 55.

6. Quoted in Robert Leighton and Griffith Thomas, *The Crossway Classic Commentaries: 1 and 2 Peter,* ed. Alister McGrath and J. I. Packer (Wheaton, Ill.: Crossway, 1999), 39.

7. I. Howard Marshall, *The IVP New Testament Commentary Series: 1 Peter,* ed. Grant R. Osborne (Downers Grove, Ill.: InterVarsity Press, 1991), 43.

Exercises

Review

1. Read 1 Peter 1:6–9; Genesis 22:1–19; Psalm 56; Daniel 12:3; Habakkuk 3:17–19; Matthew 5:10–16; Romans 5:3–5; 8:14–18; 12:18; 1 Corinthians 2:12–16; 2 Corinthians 4:16–18; 2 Timothy 3:12; Hebrews 12; James 1:2–8; 1 Peter 2:12; and 1 Peter 4:12–16. Based on these verses, what should be our attitude toward persecution and suffering?

2. Discuss the quotes from Scot McKnight on pages 27 and 28–29 in light of your perceptions of how the modern-day church interacts with the world.

3. Why would anyone cast her lot with a Savior who assures her that following Him faithfully will cause her to suffer?

4. Explain what faith is and what it is not. How does faith equip us to fulfill the chief end of our lives?

5. How were the recipients of Peter's first epistle able to maintain an attitude of rejoicing in the midst of various trials?

6. What happens to faith when it is tested? How does such testing encourage believers?

7. In the light of 1 Peter 1:10–12, describe the great blessing of being born and reborn on this side of the cross.

Application

1. Review your memory verses from the previous lesson. Then begin memorizing one or more of the following:

   > Psalm 56:3–4
   > Daniel 12:3
   > Hebrews 12:1–3

2. This week, use Daniel 12:3; Habakkuk 3:17–19; Matthew 5:10–16; and/or Hebrews 12 to help you pray for an attitude of rejoicing in the midst of various trials. Use 1 Peter 1:10–12 to help you thank God for the great blessing of being born and reborn on this side of the cross.

3. Have you ever been persecuted because you are a Christian? If you answered no, go to question 4. If you an-

swered yes, describe what happened to you. Do you believe the persecution you suffered was due more to the offense of the gospel or to the offense of your behavior? Do you need to repent and ask forgiveness from anyone because of offensive behavior on your part? If so, do it now. If you were persecuted for righteousness sake, how does Peter's commendation and exhortation of these suffering first-century believers encourage you?

4. If you have never been persecuted because you are a Christian, prayerfully seek discernment from God regarding whether you are too much at peace with the world. Discuss this lesson with your pastor, a leader of your church, or a mature Christian friend or mentor and ask him or her to help you determine whether you need to make any changes in your routine lifestyle.

Digging Deeper

1. In the light of 1 Peter 1:10–12, study and comment upon these insightful words from the great Lutheran commentator, R. C. H. Lenski: "The whole New Testament gospel rests on the Spirit's Old Testament testimony that was made through the Old Testament prophets. Cancel that testimony, and you remove the basis of the gospel of Christ" (quoted in Simon J. Kistemaker, *New Testament Commentary: Exposition of Peter* [Grand Rapids: 1996], 56).

Primary Passage
1 Peter 1:13-21

Supplementary Passages
Leviticus 11:44-45; 19:1-2; 20:7
Proverbs 9:10; 8:11-20
Matthew 5:48
Luke 12:4-5
Romans 6; 12:1-2
1 Corinthians 2:12-16
2 Corinthians 5:10-15; 7:1
Ephesians 5:15-18
Colossians 3:1-4
Titus 2:11-14
James 2:14-26
1 John 2:3-6

Before reading the lesson material, please read the primary Scripture passage listed above and as many of the supplementary passages as time allows. Then briefly summarize in your notebook what you have read. (Do not go into detail. Limit your summary to a brief description of the people, events, and/or ideas discussed in the passages.)

3

The Shift from Doctrine to Practice

The indicative of what God has done for us (and in us) precedes the imperative of what we are called to do for Him.   —Edmund Clowney

I love to diagram sentences in my spare time. But most of you probably don't. Some of you may be rolling your eyes and thinking, *I had a hunch she was a bit strange.* Others of you may shiver in horror at the very idea that someone might actually enjoy such a dry, technical task.

My daughter, Cinnamon, experienced a similar horror with Algebra II. She couldn't make heads or tails out of her textbook, didn't believe she would ever have "any use for this stuff," and was in danger of failing the class. Then a young friend of mine (who had recently received a science degree from MIT) volunteered to tutor her. The first thing he said was, "Cinnamon, math is our friend." Then he went on to show her why. She got the message and passed the class. She's still not a "math whiz," but she knows enough to use mathematical principles effectively in her daily life.

As we begin this lesson, you need to know that "grammar is our friend" too. Not only does it equip us to communicate effectively, but it helps us to recognize patterns of truth in Scripture. Edmund Clowney's words quoted above are a case in point. But if you can't recall the meanings of the grammatical terms he uses, you won't get the point. So let's review.

Verbs are words that express the action in a sentence. They also express the nature of that action through tense, voice, and mood. Tense reveals when the action takes place (past, present, or future). Voice reveals whether the subject of the sentence does the action (active voice) or is acted upon (passive voice). And mood reveals the intent of the sentence: The indicative mood makes a statement or asks a question; the imperative mood makes a request or issues a command; and the subjunctive mood expresses a possible or hypothetical condition, not a fact.

Now if you'll read Clowney's words again, they will make more sense. He's describing an encouraging feature of God's revelation in Scripture: The imperatives (commands) of Christian living typically follow the indicatives (factual statements) of God's gracious actions on our behalf. Before the writers of Scripture exhort us to behave in certain ways, they prepare us for obedience by describing what God has done for us.

Some of the clearest examples of this feature of Scripture are in the writings of Paul. Most of his letters contain easily spotted transition verses that mark a shift in his teaching from doctrine (who God is and what He has done) to practice (what we are to do in response to who God is and what He has done). Paul, who was an orderly, logical thinker, typically highlighted transition verses by using the word *therefore*. When we see a "therefore" in one of Paul's letters, we should always pause to consider what it is there for. If it is followed by verses full of imperatives, it may mark a shift from doctrine to practice. If so, it calls us to quit thinking in terms of simply knowing God's truth and start thinking in terms of living it out.[1]

Not all the writers of Scripture organize their material in the way that Paul does, but they all base imperatives upon indicative truth about God. Whenever the writers of Scripture call us to obedience, their exhortations are based on God's gracious actions toward us.

Peter's Transition
(1 Peter 1:13)

The apostle Peter was no exception. He even used a transition verse, much like Paul did, to alert his readers to an imminent shift from doctrine to practice. "Therefore," he says, "prepare ["gird," NASB 1977] your minds for action, keep sober in spirit, fix your hope completely on the grace to be brought to you at the revelation of Jesus Christ." Then he proceeds to pack the rest of his letter with imperative verbs. What is Peter's *therefore* there for? To encourage his readers to look back to the preceding indicatives before they wade into those upcoming imperatives.

Peter knew that his first-century readers would find those imperatives a little unsettling. He was about to command them to glorify God in their unfriendly culture by behaving in ways guaranteed to produce more painful sparks. He was about to assure them that the various trials they had been enduring weren't likely to end. In fact, they were sure to intensify. And he was about to warn them that their heretofore worthy walk could quickly disintegrate into an unworthy limp if they lost sight of the doctrine he had already taught them.

Peter had affirmed that their faith and hope were in the God who is sovereign, mighty, and good. He had explained that their faith was strong because it was grounded in knowledge of who God is and what He has done. He had said that their living hope was encouraging because it was anchored in God's gracious promise of a sure inheritance. He had proclaimed that their trials were necessary and beneficial and would result in praise, glory, and honor at the revelation of Jesus Christ. And he had reminded them of how blessed they were to be born and reborn on this side of the cross.

All that they needed to respond well to the upcoming imperatives was a rock-solid grip on those unfailing indicatives. They had everything they needed in their faith to live as God-honoring lights in the midst of their fallen culture. God's grace was sufficient to fuel their obedience. And what was true for them is true also for us. Wayne Grudem expressed it well when he said, "New Testament 'hope' . . . is much stronger than the vague sense of 'wish for' or 'dream about.' It [conveys] a sense of confident expectation, an expectation strong enough for one to act on the basis of it."[2]

A few weeks ago, I boarded an airplane and sat next to a woman who was clearly distressed. Her red eyes darted nervously one moment and stared vacantly the next while her husband kept compassionately patting her knee. As we taxied, took off, and climbed to our cruising altitude, she periodically covered her face and cried quietly into her hands. Finally, she looked at me and said, "I'm not crazy. We're on our way to our son's memorial service." I murmured condolences and asked her for details. Her son, a young lawyer traveling overseas, had been killed the week before in a terrorist bomb blast. He left a wife and young children in addition to his bereaved parents.

Not sure where to begin in trying to comfort her, I asked her if she was a Christian. Her eyes flashed momentarily as she snapped, "Yes. But I am so angry at God. This isn't fair. This isn't fair at all." I immediately thought of how differently my friend D. J. had responded to a similar tragedy. What made the difference between these two Christian women? Why did one turn *to* God in *faith* in the face of disaster and the other turned *on* God in *anger?*

Peter has told us. One had a rock-solid grip on Scripture's unfailing indicatives. What she knew about God and His purposes gave her hope and a confident expectation—the ingredients of strength that equip us to act as God-honoring lights in this world. As I talked with the other, I discovered she didn't. Her view of God wasn't biblical. She saw Him primarily as the source of her self-defined well-being and happiness. She thought He had let her down, and her faith was in shambles. Consequently, her behavior did not glorify God in this world the way D. J.'s did.

The difference between these two women underscored in my mind the importance of making an effort to get to know God. The woman on the airplane wasn't in any mood for a lecture about God's sovereign control over all circumstances of life. And yet that's where the only real comfort lies. D. J. could avail herself of that comfort because she knew God very well *before* tragedy struck. Holding on to the indicatives she had already learned equipped her to glorify God in difficult circumstances.

Peter's transition verse captures the essence of distinctively Christian living. It tells us that glorifying God in this world is primarily a matter of mind and heart management.[3] Peter says that the holy behavior that glorifies God begins with girding our minds for action, keeping sober in spirit, and fixing our hope on God's grace revealed in and through Jesus Christ.

Peter's first-century readers understood the word *gird* to refer to the practice of tucking the skirt of their typical garment into their belts in preparation for hard work. But in our day, hard work is rarely done in a skirt. So, if Peter were writing his letter today, he might have said something like "roll up the sleeves of your mind" or "buckle down to think."

Either phrase would express to us what "gird" conveyed in the first century—that glorifying God in the world begins with preparing our minds for disciplined thinking. Jesus said that the great and foremost commandment is to love the Lord with all of our hearts, souls, and minds (Matthew 22:37). Paul exhorted the Romans to be transformed by the renewing of their minds and advised the Colossians to set their minds on the things above, not on the things that are on the earth (Romans 12:2; Colossians 3:2). The book of Proverbs extols the virtues of applying our minds to acquiring knowledge of God (Proverbs 18:15; 22:17). And Isaiah assures us that God will keep the "steadfast of mind" in perfect peace because they trust in Him (Isaiah 26:3).

The best way for Christians to gird their minds for action is by actively cultivating an addiction to Scripture. Rolling up the sleeves of our minds and buckling down to think about God and the things He has done equips us to trust Him enough to obey Him. And trusting Him enough to obey Him produces the holy behavior that glorifies God and enhances our joy.

Peter tells us that girding our minds for action helps us manage our hearts by giving us sober spirits. Disciplined study of Scripture impresses us with the seriousness of our high calling in Christ. It teaches us that we have been redeemed for the purpose of doing good works that glorify God and that fulfilling our purpose requires constant vigilance against temptations to sin. It teaches us that we are earthen vessels, inadequate in ourselves to defend against sin and glorify God in our behavior. And it teaches us that we must rely upon God's Holy Spirit to strengthen us for the task we've been given.

Christians who manage their minds and hearts well are

the ones who quite naturally fix their hope on God's grace revealed in and through Jesus Christ. They know that God's grace did much more than save them. They have learned from God's Word that grace also equips them for obedience and guarantees that His promises will come to fruition. They understand that God's grace underlies everything He has done for them in the past, is doing for them in the present, and will do for them in the future. Their salvation, their service, and their inheritance all depend upon Him, not upon them.[4] Fixing their hope on the grace revealed in and through Jesus Christ allows them to move from doctrine to practice so that God gets the glory.

An Impossible Mission?
(1 Peter 1:14–16)
Peter followed his transition verse with a general exhortation to holiness: "As obedient children," he said, "do not be conformed to the former lusts which were yours in your ignorance, but like the Holy One who called you, be holy yourselves also in all your behavior; because it is written, 'You shall be holy, for I am holy.' " Stop and think about Peter's words for a moment. Does his exhortation strike you as a distressingly impossible mission? Are you so aware of your fallen sinfulness that you can't picture yourself being "holy in all your behavior"? If so, rest assured, Peter knows where you're coming from.

The man who commanded you to be holy in all your behavior had sinned greatly himself—so greatly that he nearly succumbed to despair. But God's grace sustained Peter during the dark, dismal days following his denial of Christ. And then God's grace forgave him, restored him, and mightily used him in kingdom service. By the time Peter wrote his first epistle, he had a vise grip on the Bible's indicative truth about grace. He knew that God's grace had done more than deliver him from sin's ghastly penalty. It had also delivered him from sin's brutal authority. Peter understood, intellectually and experientially, that God's grace not only saves us for the purpose of doing good works that glorify Him (see Matthew 5:16; Ephesians 1:3–14; 2:8–10). It also equips us to do those good works (2 Corinthians 9:8).

The good works that glorify God fall into two basic categories: nonconformity to our former manner of life and conformity to Christ. In short, we are to obey God's commands to mortify[5] sin in our lives and to pattern our daily activities after the word and example of Christ. However, obeying God isn't simply a matter of determined human effort. It requires us to depend on His gracious enabling. The secret of being "holy in all [our] behavior" is tightening our grip on this essential indicative: The power enabling obedience to God's commands comes from the reality of our union with Christ. Even though as redeemed fallen sinners, we remain distressingly vulnerable to sin's temptation, as believers united with Christ, we are no longer subject to sin's authority.

G. K. Chesterton, though speaking in a different context, illustrated the way sin operates in the life of a believer with this memorable word picture. He said, "If a rhinoceros were to enter this restaurant right now, there is no denying he would have great power here. But I should be the first to rise and assure him that he had no authority whatever."[6]

Kris Lundgaard in *The Enemy Within* quotes Chesterton and goes on to say that "the law of sin in believers is like Chesterton's rhino. The only moral, authoritative rule over believers is the kingdom and reign of God. Indwelling sin is a usurper to the throne, who, like the rhino, can at times force himself on us. Even though we rise and tell him he has no authority, he can push us around the restaurant."[7]

Sin is a powerful foe, and we should never underestimate its insidious ability to deceive, intimidate, and bully us into submission. But neither should we forget that it has no authority to command our obedience. Salvation transferred us from the domain of darkness to the kingdom of God's beloved Son (Colossians 1:13). The Son's power surpasses all other power, and His dominion extends over all of creation (see Ephesians 1:18–23).

When God's Holy Spirit came to indwell us, we became slaves of God rather than slaves of sin. Our Lord's authority to command our obedience and His power to enable us to obey Him is greater than anything sin can throw at us. When sin usurps authority and starts to push us around, we can and should start pushing back—in the power of the Holy Spirit and on God's authority.

Paul emphasized sin's lack of authority over believers when he reminded the Romans that they had been united with Christ in His death and resurrection (Romans 6:1–5). Therefore, "our old self was crucified with Him, in order that our body of sin might be done away with, so that we would no longer be slaves to sin" (Romans 6:6). When we are placed in union with Christ and given the gift of God's indwelling Spirit, we are freed from sin's bondage and are no longer subject to its authority. However, because we remain fallen beings, we can and frequently do allow ourselves to be deceived, intimidated, or bullied by sin. When we behave in such ways, we don't glorify God. That's why Paul went on to say:

> Even so consider yourselves to be dead to sin, but alive to God in Christ Jesus. Therefore do not let sin reign in your mortal body that you obey its lusts, and do not go on presenting the members of your body to sin as instruments of unrighteousness; but present yourselves to God as those alive from the dead, and your members as instruments of righteousness to God. For sin shall not be master over

you, for you are not under law but under grace. (Romans 6:11-14)

God saved us by grace for the purpose of our doing good works that glorify Him (Matthew 5:16; Ephesians 2:10). We do those good works by obeying the imperatives recorded in Scripture. Obedience to those imperatives is empowered by the indicative truths about God that are also recorded in Scripture. Tightening our grip on those truths and drawing strength from His Spirit fulfills God's purposes for our salvation by giving Him glory and enhancing our joy.

Grasping God's truth and drawing on His Spirit's power involve managing our minds and hearts. When we roll up the sleeves of our minds and buckle down to think about Scripture, we learn to recognize and resist temptations. The Bible defines sin graphically and gives us specific instructions about how to combat it. The better we know God's Word, the better equipped we will be to mortify sin in our lives.

The ladies in my Tuesday discussion group in Albuquerque never talk about "girding their minds for action." They don't even refer to "rolling up the sleeves of their minds" or "buckling down to think." They speak of *"marinating* our minds in Scripture." I like that phrase because it captures the pervasive influence God's Word should have on every aspect of life. Marinating our minds and hearts in the Scriptures equips us to pattern our daily activities after the example of Christ. The Bible tells us that Jesus Christ always did the will of the Father (John 4:34; 5:30; 6:38; 8:28; 17:4). It also asserts that it is the record of God's revealed will for our lives (Psalm 119:105; 2 Timothy 3:15-17; 2 Peter 1:3-4). Therefore, growing in Christlikeness by doing God's will results only from understanding and living out, in the power of the Holy Spirit, the truths found in Scripture.

When our minds and hearts are managed by Scripture, we will naturally fix our hope on God's grace revealed in and through Jesus Christ. And we'll rely on His power to fuel our transition from doctrine to practice so that God gets the glory.

Living Hope Motivates Heart and Mind Management
(1 Peter 1:17–21)

Peter knew that effective heart and mind management takes effort on our part. And he also knew that most redeemed sinners aren't inclined to expend effort unless they are properly motivated. So he moves immediately from exhortation to stimulation. He deftly displays how living hope energizes pursuit of holiness when he says, "If you address as Father the One who impartially judges according to each one's work, conduct yourselves in fear during the time of your stay on earth" (v. 17).

Living hope lights a fire under righteous behavior because it trusts God to do what He has said He will do. We can know (for a fact, without doubt) that we will receive our inheritance because Scripture reveals God to be an impartial Judge who never permits a miscarriage of justice. Scripture's indicatives teach us that on judgment day, He will exact the wages of sin from those who have broken His law. We can be sure that no condemned sinner will succeed in cajoling or bribing Him into commuting his or her deserved sentence. However, we who have been redeemed and adopted into God's family will escape His righteous wrath on that day. Why? Because our unpayable debt has been paid in full by Another. God's justice, in our case, was fully satisfied in the atonement of Christ.

Contemplating the righteous justice displayed at the cross spurs us to conduct ourselves "in fear" during our stay on this earth. Peter says that this fear motivates righteous behavior, but not because we're afraid God will rescind our inheritance if we don't behave well. The Bible tells us that our inheritance is ours by right of what Christ has done for us, not by right of what we do for God. The fear that motivates righteous behavior is one that desires, above all, to honor the One who has saved us. It is a fear born out of gratitude, reverence, and awe. It behaves well because it respects and appreciates God's power and love.

We can be sure of what Peter meant when he used the word *fear* by reading the verses that follow. He doesn't support his command with dire threats of what God will do to us if we fail to comply. Rather, he revels in the glories of God's gracious salvation:

> You were not redeemed with perishable things like silver or gold from your futile way of life inherited from your forefathers, but with precious blood, as of a lamb unblemished and spotless, the blood of Christ. For He was foreknown before the foundation of the world, but has appeared in these last times for the sake of you who through Him are believers in God, who raised Him from the dead and gave Him glory, so that your faith and hope are in God. (1:18–21)

The living hope of God's chosen children rests in the fact that before the foundation of the world, God planned to redeem us through the precious blood of His Son. Before times eternal, He chose us in Him to be a holy and blameless gift for His Son (John 17:6–24; Ephesians 1:4; Titus 1:1–3). And at the right time in human history, He sent His Son into the world in the likeness of men to atone for our sin and redeem us from its power (Philippians 2:6–8; Romans 6:5–9).

Our living hope is rooted and grounded in what He has accomplished. Our living hope spurs us to exercise faith in pursuit of holiness—by trusting God to do what He has promised to do. And our living hope fosters the gratitude, reverence, and awe that spur us to move from doctrine to practice so that God gets the glory.

Notes

1. For a few examples of transition verses in Paul's letters, see Romans 12:1; Ephesians 4:1; Philippians 2:1; and Colossians 2:6.

2. Wayne Grudem, *The Tyndale New Testament Commentaries: 1 Peter* (Grand Rapids: Eerdmans, 1988), 76.

3. Matthew Henry, *Matthew Henry's Commentary on the Whole Bible,* vol. 6, *Acts to Revelation* (Peabody, Mass.: Hendrickson, 1991), 814.

4. For a full explanation of how God's grace saves, equips, and assures believers, see Jerry Bridges, *Transforming Grace: Living Confidently in God's Unfailing Love* (Colorado Springs: NavPress, 1991).

5. In theological terms, to mortify something means "to put it to death." Thus Christians are called to pursue holiness by putting sin to death in their lives. Ironically, the mortification of sin in the life of a believer turns out to be a continual process. Since our redeemed fallen natures have not yet been glorified, we remain highly vulnerable to sin's allure throughout our lives here on earth. Therefore, sins we may think we have successfully mortified have a way of springing back into life. Paul's words

in 1 Corinthians 10:12 serve as a word to the wise: "Let him who thinks he stands take heed that he does not fall." The pursuit of holiness doesn't allow us to drop our guard in the ongoing battle to mortify sin. It requires constant vigilance.

6. Kris Lundgaard, *The Enemy Within: Straight Talk about the Power and Defeat of Sin* (Phillipsburg, N.J.: P&R, 1998), 29.

7. Ibid.

Exercises

Review

1. Distinguish between an indicative and an imperative. Then describe the significance of this distinction for the passage of Scripture discussed in this lesson.

2. What clues help you recognize 1 Peter 1:13 as a transition verse? What should you do immediately upon recognizing it as a transition verse? How will doing this help you understand the meaning of this verse and the verses that follow?

3. How does fixing our hope on God's grace help us fulfill our chief end of glorifying God and enjoying Him forever? How do girding our minds for action and keeping sober in spirit help us fix our hope on God's grace?

4. Identify the two categories of the good works God calls us to do. Then explain the secret of being holy in all your behavior.

5. Read Romans 6 carefully and explain in your own words the important truths Paul presents about Christian living. How does Paul's teaching in Romans 6 relate to Peter's teaching in 1 Peter 1:13–16?

6. Describe the connection Peter draws between pursuit of holiness and living hope. How does understanding this connection help us to move from doctrine to practice so that God gets the glory?

Application

1. Review your memory verses from the previous lesson. Then begin memorizing one or more of the following:

   Matthew 5:48
   Colossians 3:1–4
   1 Peter 1:13–16

2. This week in your prayer time, use Isaiah 40:28–31; 41:9–13; Ephesians 1:3–14; and Colossians 3:1–4 to help you reflect on the grandeur of God's glorious grace. Allow these passages to stimulate prayers of thanksgiving, praise, confession, and supplication.

3. List the routine activities in which you participate during an average week. Then go through your list and identify the activities that roll up the sleeves of your mind and require you to buckle down to think about God's nature and actions. Identify the actions that help you develop sober-minded attitudes toward your life in this world. Finally, identify the actions that "fix your hope completely on the grace to be brought to you at the revelation of Jesus Christ" (1 Peter 1:13). Analyze your list to determine whether your daily activities are helping

or hindering you to fulfill your chief end of glorifying God and enjoying Him forever. What changes do you need to make in your daily activities in order to pursue your chief end more effectively? When will you begin making these changes? Who loves you enough to encourage you and hold you accountable to make these changes? When will you request their assistance?

4. Does Peter's exhortation in 1:14–16 seem like an impossible mission to you? If so, how do the indicatives of what God has done for you and in you discussed in this lesson encourage you to pursue obedience to his exhortation?

Digging Deeper

1. Dr. Edmund Clowney said, "The imperatives of Christian living always begin with 'therefore,' " meaning that they are always preceded by the indicatives of what God has done for us. If I were to add that the indicatives of what God has done for us are always followed by imperatives of Christian living, would you agree? Explain, supporting your thoughts with Scripture.

2. Read *The Enemy Within* by Kris Lundgaard. Then use what you learn to develop a discipling tool (a lesson plan, outline, chart, diagram, etc.) that will help other believers understand the power and defeat of sin.

Primary Passage
1 Peter 1:22–2:10

Supplementary Passages
Exodus 19:1–6
Psalms 34:8; 118:22; 119:103
Isaiah 8:11–15; 28:16; 40:6–8
Hosea 1–2
Matthew 16:13–19
John 13:1–14:7
Romans 12:1–2
1 Corinthians 3:16; 6:19–20; 13:4–8a
Ephesians 2:19–22; 5:1–2
Philippians 2:1–18
Colossians 1:13–14
Hebrews 13:15–16
1 John 1:5–7; 3:1–3

Before reading the lesson material, please read the primary Scripture passage listed above and as many of the supplementary passages as time allows. Then briefly summarize in your notebook what you have read. (Do not go into detail. Limit your summary to a brief description of the people, events, and/or ideas discussed in the passages.)

4

The Attractiveness of God's People

Jesus did not die just to save us from the penalty of sin, nor even just to make us holy in our standing before God. He died to purify for Himself a people eager to please Him, a people eager to be transformed into His likeness. —Jerry Bridges

Whenever Frank and I have out-of-town guests, we enjoy taking them sightseeing. Albuquerque, with its rich multi-cultural heritage, boasts an intriguing array of attractions. And a few of these attractions are just plain odd. One of the oddest is a house so unusual that it sometimes stops traffic.

Situated in the midst of a old neighborhood filled with traditional homes, it is shaped like a submarine . . . or maybe a caterpillar . . . or maybe a pregnant cigar. Frank and I can't quite decide. We love including that house in our sightseeing tours and watching the expressions on our friends' faces. None of them can quite decide what it looks like either. Most don't even try. They just grab their cameras and mumble something like, "Aunt Bertha will never believe this!"

While that house has become an Albuquerque *attraction* because it's just plain odd, directly across from it stands a house that is *attractive* because it's just plain appealing. It is constructed of rocks—hundreds of rocks—of all shapes, sizes, and colors held together by strong, solid mortar. With no two rocks exactly alike, they form a beautiful kaleidoscope of stunning patterns and hues as the house is viewed from different perspectives. The house boasts large rooms, wide windows, and stately chimneys—exuding warmth, charm, and undeniable hominess. It's a dead ringer for those warm, fuzzy places depicted in Thomas Kinkade's paintings.

Interestingly, in all the years Frank and I have included those two houses on our sightseeing tours, no one has ever asked us if the odd, submarine-caterpillar-pregnant cigar house is for sale. But when our friends see the rock house, they usually do. The odd house stops folks in their tracks and makes them reach for their cameras. But the rock house warms their hearts and begs them to call their real-estate agents.

There are other houses, of course, on the same street. But although I have seen them dozens of times, I can't describe them for you. Perhaps that's because there's nothing distinctive about them. Only two houses get noticed on that particular street: one very odd, the other so very appealing.

I thought about those two houses this week as I was studying the great truths contained in 1 Peter 1:22–2:10. In these verses, we hear Peter describe how God builds His children into a distinctive people. He shapes them through the work of His Word and His Spirit into a spiritual house that doesn't blend in with the sinful culture around them. Through the grace of redemption and sanctification, He erects and adorns a dwelling place for Himself that stands out from the crowd. He takes "living stones" (2:5) of all shapes, sizes, and colors and binds them together with the strong, solid mortar of His gospel of grace. The spiritual house that He builds has been clearly designed to *attract* the lost sinners around us by proclaiming the excellencies of its Master Builder.

In our last lesson, we heard Peter exhort us to set our minds on the indicatives of what God has done in us and for us as we obey the imperatives He sets before us. And in this lesson, we'll hear Peter explain that God doesn't command us to be holy in all our behavior so that we'll be odd. Rather, He commands us to be holy so that we'll be appealing. The appeal of God's spiritual house lies in the way it displays the dynamic connection between love and God's truth while reflecting the purposeful beauty of His spiritual architecture.

The Dynamic Connection Between Love and God's Truth
(1 Peter 1:22–2:3)

Peter may well have stopped at this point in writing his letter and thought back to the night before Jesus died. He might have relived the breathtaking moment when Jesus arose from the table, girded Himself like the lowest of slaves, and set about washing the feet of His proud disciples. Perhaps Peter heard once again his Master say that He was giving them an example and that they should do for each other what He had done for them. They were to love one another as He had loved them, reflecting the reality of their redemptive, transforming union with Jesus Christ, God's incarnation of truth (see John 13:1–35; 14:6).

I picture Peter tightening his grip on his quill and leaning over the parchment with intensity etched in every line of his face. It was essential that those to whom he was writing understand the importance of loving each other in the midst of their difficulties. God had equipped them, by His grace, to reflect the love of Christ in their relationships with one another. But the pressures of persecution have a way of short-circuiting witness. The stress of outside attack could easily lead them to snipe at each other instead of reflecting Christlikeness in their love for each other.

If they were to be an attractive, inviting spiritual house, one that proclaimed the excellencies of its Master Builder, they needed to grasp and display the dynamic connection between love and God's truth. I'm sure Peter prayed for just the right words as he resumed writing his letter:

> Since you have in obedience to the truth purified your souls for a sincere love of the brethren, fervently love one another from the heart, for you have been born again not of seed which is perishable but imperishable, that is, through the living and abiding word of God. For,
>
> > "All flesh is like grass,
> > And all its glory like the flower of grass.
> > The grass withers,
> > And the flower falls off,
> > But the word of the Lord endures forever."
>
> And this is the word which was preached to you. Therefore, putting aside all malice and all deceit and hypocrisy and envy and all slander, like newborn babies, long for the pure milk of the word, so that by it you may grow in respect to salvation, if you have tasted the kindness of the Lord. (1 Peter 1:22–2:3)

Peter affirmed that the power of the living, abiding Word of God is what equips us to fervently love one another. God's truth takes root in our hearts when we are saved.

There it is cultivated and nurtured by His indwelling Spirit. There it fulfills its purpose of teaching, rebuking, correcting, and training us for effective service (James 1:21; 2 Corinthians 1:12; 2 Timothy 3:16–17). And there it helps us develop deep love for each other. I. Howard Marshall explains that "the motive and ability to obey the commandment to love flow from the new birth and the new life that it opens up."[1]

Loving each other (as described in 1 Corinthians 13:4–8a) is difficult for us fallen sinners, even for us *redeemed* fallen sinners. That's because we all tend to think that the world revolves around us. When someone steps on our toes, we're not likely to ask if *he* hurt *his* foot. But God's Word commands us to put the interests of others ahead of our own. He wants us to be more concerned about that blundering oaf's foot than we are about our own toes. Why? Because the ability to love like that comes only from His Holy Spirit. And living out that kind of love reflects His work in us, which glorifies God. Demonstrating that kind of love in the body of Christ is particularly important. It heightens the distinctiveness that makes us attractive to the world around us.

Peter says that we fulfill the command to love one another by doing two things: putting aside all malice, guile, hypocrisy, envy, and slander; and longing for the pure milk of the Word like newborn babies. We must put aside the behaviors he mentions because they are incompatible with living out love. And we must long for the pure milk of the Word because its truths nourish us so that we grow with respect to salvation.

Malice is an attitude of ill will that seeks to harm others. Its destructive intent locks love out of relationships. Guile is another word for deceit. It speaks or acts to deceive and thus destroys the trust upon which love is based. Hypocrisy pretends to be something it's not. It creates a dishonest atmosphere in which love cannot breathe. Envy is jealous of the blessings of others. It chokes the life out of love because of its selfishness. And slander is speaking evil of other people. It starves love by refusing to nourish it. Peter says nurturing such unloving behavior isn't consistent with truth and thus mars our witness.

Of course, we are quite prone to engage in unloving behavior when we are under attack. Persecution and trials tempt us to succumb to a self-centered defensiveness that jettisons all thought of loving the brethren. Peter says the best way to fight off that temptation is to develop a taste for the pure milk of the Word. Understanding and living out the truths found in Scripture will help us put off those hateful behaviors and put on fervent love for each other as we grow with respect to salvation. Peter exhorts us to long for the pure milk of the Word like little babies. Think for a moment about that vivid word picture.

Have you ever been caught with a hungry baby and without any milk? I have, and believe me, it wasn't fun. I had my infant daughter with me on campus, and when feeding time rolled around she started to fuss. I reached into my bag and frantically realized I had forgotten her bottle! She wasn't about to be fooled by the pacifier and had no interest at all in being held, walked, or talked to. She wanted her milk, and she wanted it then. Nothing else in the world would satisfy her.

Do we desire God's Word with that kind of intensity? If we did, Peter says we'd reflect the dynamic connection between love and God's truth. The taste of God's kindness toward us, expressed in the truth of His love, mercy, and grace, whets our appetites for more of His truth. The more of His truth we learn and apply, the more we grow and mature in Christlikeness. The more Christlike we are, the more devoted we are to loving each other. The more we love each other, the more we're built up into an attractive spiritual house that reflects the excellencies of its Master Builder.

The Purposeful Beauty of God's Spiritual Architecture
(1 Peter 2:4–10)

I believe that the rock house in Albuquerque is so attractive because its architecture and structure reflect its purpose so beautifully. Even a quick look at that house tells you that it is a home. Its appearance proclaims that it was designed and built to protect, comfort, and nurture somebody's family. Closer scrutiny validates and intensifies that first impression. And since all human beings seem to crave warm family relationships, the hominess of that house is very appealing.

In much the same way, even a quick look at God's blueprints for His spiritual house reveal that He designed it and built it to proclaim His excellencies. And since all human beings are created for God and are restless until they find their rest in Him,[2] God's spiritual house will exude a certain appeal, even to the most hardened of sinners.

The attractiveness of God's spiritual house derives from the way its architecture and structure reflect the excellencies of God's plan of redemption. The cornerstone that supports the whole building is Jesus Christ, God's only Son, who secured our redemption (Ephesians 2:20; 1 Peter 2:6–7a). The foundation extending from that cornerstone is the living witness of the apostles and prophets who proclaimed the gospel on both sides of the cross (Ephesians 2:20). The superstructure is composed of believers in Christ, who work out what salvation worked in them in their worship, service, and evangelistic encounters (Philippians 2:12–16).

Peter describes all believers as "living stones" built into a house that rests securely on the Living Stone.

> And coming to Him as a living stone, which has been rejected by men, but is choice and precious

in the sight of God, you also, as living stones, are being built up as a spiritual house for a holy priesthood, to offer up spiritual sacrifices acceptable to God through Jesus Christ. For this is contained in Scripture:

> "Behold, I lay in Zion a choice stone, a precious corner stone,
> And he who believes in Him will not be disappointed."

This precious value, then, is for you who believe; but for those who disbelieve,

> "The stone which the builders rejected,
> This became the very corner stone,"

and,

> "A stone of stumbling and a rock of offense";

for they stumble because they are disobedient to the word, and to this doom they were also appointed. But you are a chosen race, a royal priesthood, a holy nation, a people for God's own possession, so that you may proclaim the excellencies of Him who has called you out of darkness into His marvelous light; for you once were not a people, but now you are the people of God; you had not received mercy, but now you have received mercy. (1 Peter 2:4–10)

Throughout the ages, God has given His people an attractive distinction by dwelling among them. His dwelling among them has been closely related to His revelation of truth and has grown progressively intimate as His revelation has become more and more personal. At first, God simply revealed His existence and will to key leaders like Abraham, Isaac, Jacob, and Joseph. Then He manifested

His presence among His people during critical times through unusual physical phenomena such as burning bushes and pillars of cloud and fire.

Next, God settled among them in a portable tent called the tabernacle and a beautiful fixed structure known as the temple. Then when the time was right, He sent His Son in their likeness to live in their midst and accomplish redemption. Once the Son's work was done, He returned to the Father and joined Him in sending the Spirit to indwell believers from all nations and races. Perhaps the greatest blessing associated with being born and reborn on this side of the cross is that God now dwells in His people instead of with them.

But to whom much is given, must is also required. Our mission as God's spiritual house is to function as a holy priesthood, offering "spiritual sacrifices acceptable to God through Jesus Christ" (2:5). Scripture teaches us that spiritual sacrifices are offered in various ways. We are to offer God our bodies (Romans 12:1), our gifts (Philippians 4:18), our praises (Hebrews 13:15), and our service (Hebrews 13:16). In other words, He wants all that we are and all that we have. We are to dedicate our whole lives to the cause of Christ. That's because all that we are and all that we have come from His gracious atonement.

The precious cornerstone upon whom we rely will not disappoint us. His grace equips us and sustains us as we fulfill the mission God gives us: to exalt Him with our worship, edify one another with our teaching and service, and to evangelize the lost with our proclamation of His gospel. Peter Davids asserts in his commentary that "Christians are to 'publish abroad' the mighty works of God, which include both his activity in creation and his miracle of redemption in the life, death, resurrection, and revelation of Jesus Christ. . . . This heraldic praise is their reason for existing."[3] However, we cannot accomplish our mission without divine assistance. Scot McKnight says it well: "All true Christian development is the result of knowing God the Father, participating in the work of the Son, and submitting to the guidance of the Holy Spirit."[4]

Peter issues a grave warning to those who disbelieve before summarizing God's beautiful purpose for His spiritual house. Those who reject God's precious cornerstone and refuse to build their lives upon Him will find Him to be a "stone of stumbling and a rock of offense" (2:8). Christians, however, should not be alarmed by the world's rejection of Him and of them. Peter says these disbelievers were "appointed" by God for the doom they will reap (v. 8). Although they may bring temporary affliction into the lives of believers, God's purposes will be accomplished in spite of their actions. He will take what rebellious sinners intended for evil and use it for good.

God's people can be strong in the face of persecution because they are now what they have been since the days of Abraham: "A chosen race, a royal priesthood, a holy nation, a people for God's own possession" (v. 9). They have been called out of darkness into God's marvelous light, shown mercy, and made into a people for His possession. God has built them into an attractive spiritual house for the purpose of proclaiming His excellencies to those around them.

The rest of Peter's letter will emphasize the practical consequences of that glorious truth. He will exhort us to proclaim indicative truth about God and to do so in ways that will appeal to the real needs of lost sinners. He will urge us to rely on the power of the indwelling Spirit and to rest in the strength of our precious cornerstone. And he will assure us that no evil power will be able to thwart God's purposes for us.

Before going on to the exercises that follow, take a few moments to thank God in prayer for calling you out of darkness into His marvelous light. Thank Him for forming you into a living stone for His spiritual house. And thank Him for the privilege of proclaiming His excellencies with your words and your life.

Notes

1. I. Howard Marshall, *The IVP New Testament Commentary Series: 1 Peter,* ed. Grant R. Osborne (Downers Grove, Ill.: InterVarsity Press, 1991), 60.

2. See the first chapter of Romans and book 1 of Augustine's *Confessions.*

3. Peter H. Davids, *The New International Commentary on the New Testament: The First Epistle of Peter,* ed. Ned B. Stonehouse, F. F. Bruce, and Gordon D. Fee (Grand Rapids: Eerdmans, 1990), 93.

4. Scot McKnight, *The NIV Application Commentary: 1 Peter* (Grand Rapids: Zondervan, 1996), 120.

Exercises

Review

1. Distinctiveness can result from either oddness or appeal. In your own words, describe the difference between odd distinctiveness and appealing distinctiveness. Then explain the importance of understanding this difference to our Christian witness.

2. Read John 13:1–14:7. What unusual thing did Jesus do for His disciples in these verses? What did He say was

the reason for His actions? How did He describe Himself to them (John 14:6–7)? Do you see the dynamic connection He made between love and God's truth? If so, explain it in your own words.

3. What makes it possible for us to obey God's commands, particularly His command that we love one another? How does obeying the command to love one another enhance our testimony and witness to unbelievers?

4. What two things does Peter say we must do in order to obey the command to love one another? Discuss the necessity of doing both of these things if we want to love one another.

5. Read Ephesians 2:19–22; Philippians 2:12–16; and 1 Peter 2:6–8. Then describe the architecture of God's spiritual house. How does the architecture of God's spiritual house reflect the purpose for which it is built?

6. Describe the various ways God has been pleased to dwell with His people throughout history.

7. What are our responsibilities as God's spiritual house? What should be our attitude toward unbelievers?

Application

1. Review your memory verses from the previous lesson. Then begin memorizing one or more of the following:

   Psalm 34:8
   Ephesians 5:1–2
   1 John 1:5–7

2. This week use Psalm 119; Romans 12:1–2; 1 Corinthians 13:4–8a; Ephesians 4:25–32; and Philippians 2:1–18 to help you pray for a deeper desire for the milk of the Word and for greater ability to love your brothers and sisters in Christ.

3. Define each of the following words and explain how each stifles our love for one another:

   malice
   guile
   hypocrisy
   envy
   slander

   Which of these sins are particularly tempting for you? Find out by doing this exercise: Think back over the past several weeks and list specific occasions when you have been tempted to commit one or more of these sins. Also record whether you committed the sin(s). Then, for the next several weeks, do the same exercise.

   As soon as you have determined which of these sins are particularly tempting for you, make a specific step-by-step plan that will help you resist the temptation to commit these sins. Your plan should include memorization of relevant Scripture passages, prayer, disciplined mind management, and appropriate repentance. If you need help making your plan, seek it from one of your church leaders or from a mature Christian mentor, friend, or relative.

4. How often do you go through an entire day without eating food (aside from days set apart for fasting and prayer)? How often do you go through an entire day without reading and studying the Bible? Based on your

answers to these questions, can you say that you desire the milk of the Word like a baby desires milk? If you answered no to the last question, list several ways you can increase your desire for the Word of God. When, where, and how will you implement these ways to increase your desire for God's Word? Who loves you enough to encourage you and hold you accountable to follow through with your plans? When will you contact this person and ask for help?

Digging Deeper

1. First Peter 2:8 says that those who disbelieve "stumble because they are disobedient to the word, and to this doom they were also appointed." Wayne Grudem comments on this passage: "Peter's purpose in making this comment is to comfort his readers. He has shown that the rejection of Christ and even the hostile unbelief which confronted these Christians on every side were predicted by God long ago in the Old Testament (vv. 7–8a). Now he says that they were not only predicted but also planned by God (v. 8b) and are therefore within the scope of his sovereign and wise plan for the world. Hostile unbelief should not terrify Christians against whom it is directed, for God their Father holds it all under his control, and will bring it to an end when he deems it best. Amazing as it may seem, even the stumbling and disobedience of unbelievers have been *destined* by God" (Wayne Grudem, *The Tyndale New Testament Commentaries: 1 Peter* [Grand Rapids: Eerdmans, 1988], 106).

   Study this passage in the light of Romans 9, and describe in your own words the connection between God's absolute sovereignty and the hostile unbelief of those who reject Christ and persecute believers. What comfort do you find in this profound indicative biblical truth?

2. Most reputable commentators point out that Peter's language in 1 Peter 2:9–10 is corporate, referring to the church as the body of believers. However, many also emphasize the importance of individual believers making application of the truths contained in these verses in their personal lives. Scot McKnight, for example, says that these descriptions are states and functions of the church, "however, the function of the individual is a mirroring of the larger body, so that Christians individually enjoy the privilege of access to God" (Scot McKnight, *The NIV Application Commentary: 1 Peter* [Grand Rapids: Zondervan, 1996], 110).

   Discuss the importance of understanding these verses in a corporate sense, and also of making personal application of them.

Primary Passage
1 Peter 2:11–20

Supplementary Passages
Psalms 37; 73
Proverbs 4:20–27
Matthew 5:11–16, 38–48
John 19:10–11
Acts 4:13–20; 5:27–32
Romans 12:17–21; 13:1–7
2 Corinthians 2:14–16
Galatians 5:13–25
Ephesians 5:15–6:9
Philippians 3:20–21
Colossians 3:1–2; 3:12–4:6
1 Timothy 2:1–2
Titus 3:1–2
1 Peter 3:13–16

Before reading the lesson material, please read the primary Scripture passage listed above and as many of the supplementary passages as time allows. Then briefly summarize in your notebook what you have read. (Do not go into detail. Limit your summary to a brief description of the people, events, and/or ideas discussed in the passages.)

5

The Appeal of Free
Submission (1)

*A genuine Christian should be a walking mystery be-
cause he is surely a walking miracle. Through the leading and power of the Holy Spirit, the Christian is involved in a daily life and habit that cannot be explained.*
—A. W. Tozer

When my daughter, Cinnamon, was in midschool, one
of her favorite tee shirts had an underwater scene on the
front filled with cute little fish. All of them, except one,
were swimming in the same direction. The caption under
the picture read, "Go Against the Flow." I liked that shirt
because it said a mouthful about Christian living.

We live our lives in the company of unsaved sinners, but
we are not going in the same direction they are. We are not
intent on their purposes, consumed by their passions, or
obsessed by their fears. If you'll allow me to mix a couple
of metaphors, we are swimming upstream to the beat of a
different drummer. But because we are going against the
flow of the world, we get noticed. And because we get noticed, we often get a reaction.

"Hey," a helpful fish yells. "Do you know you're going the wrong direction?"

"Why make things so difficult?" another fish asks. "It's so much easier to swim with the group."

"Everyone swims this way," an old, wise fish advises. "You'll never get anywhere going that way."

"Turn around!" A big fish gives us a shove. "You're disturbing the current and making it hard for me to swim."

"Keep going that way," a group of thug fish assure us, "and you're gonna get hurt."

Peter knew what it was like to "swim upstream to the beat of a different drummer" in a world of lost sinners. He knew it wasn't easy. And he knew it was dangerous. But he also knew it was necessary. He knew it was the way we proclaim the excellencies of the One who has called us out of darkness into His marvelous light.

After explaining to his readers that they are living stones being built up as an attractive spiritual house for a holy priesthood, he goes on to give them the rest of the story. Their distinct attractiveness will be difficult to maintain, and it will also attract some unwelcome antagonism. Peter's readers will be sorely tempted by the world, the flesh, and the devil to change directions and go with the flow. And they will be slandered by those who would like nothing more than to see their spiritual house defaced to the point where it is no longer attractive.

Peter exhorts them to maintain their distinctiveness as the people of God by keeping their behavior excellent among unbelievers so that God will be glorified. He says they can do this by patterning their lives after the example of Christ as they relate to their rulers, their masters, their spouses, and each other in general.

They are "free men," he says. But they are to use their freedom as bond slaves of God. Such free submission to ordained authority will certainly require them to "swim upstream to the beat of a different drummer." It will certainly create an intriguing appeal and certainly attract some unwelcome antagonism. And it will certainly proclaim the excellencies of their Master Builder.

Since Peter's exhortation extends over quite a few verses, we'll take two lessons to cover it all. In this lesson, we'll look at 1 Peter 2:11–20, and in lesson 6 we'll continue with 1 Peter 2:21–3:12.

The Excellent Behavior That Glorifies God
(1 Peter 2:11–12)

Peter knew that going against the flow of the world was a daunting task even for seasoned, mature believers in Christ. So he sprinkled his exhortation to do so with some enticing encouragement. "Beloved," he said, "I urge you as aliens and strangers to abstain from fleshly lusts which wage war against the soul. Keep your behavior excellent among the Gentiles, so that in the thing in which they slander you as evildoers, they may because of your good deeds, as they observe them, glorify God in the day of visitation."

By referring to his readers as "beloved," Peter not only affirms his love for them but also reminds them that they are the beloved children of God. As such, their lives are governed by a distinctive perspective—one that understands they are "aliens and strangers" in this fallen world because their hope doesn't rest in the things of this world.

I. Howard Marshall summarizes their distinctive perspective succinctly and well: "Christians live a life of hope in this world, solidly rooted in the fact of the resurrection of Jesus and in their own experience of the new birth, and joyfully maintained despite the sufferings they undergo since these are a means of strengthening and proving their faith."[1]

Christians live in the sure knowledge that God has, in

His great mercy, caused them to be born again to a living hope, through the resurrection of Jesus Christ. Their living hope is God's guarantee of an imperishable, undefiled, unfading inheritance, reserved in heaven for them.

They know that no matter how much their lifestyles grate on their culture and no matter how many sparks are thrown off in the process, they are protected by God's power through their faith in Christ for a salvation to be revealed in the last time. They know that trials serve the dual purpose of refining impurities out of their faith while strengthening their hope as they depend on God's Spirit. They know that nothing can rob them of their inheritance. And so they rejoice in the midst of their trials.

Their distinctive perspective doesn't lead them to withdraw from the world. Rather, it spurs them to active engagement. Although Christians are children of God, whose true home is in heaven, they live in this world as their Father's ambassadors.

Their distinctive lifestyles, which cause them to get noticed and sometimes attacked, throw open doors of testimony and witness. Peter tells them to maintain their distinction by doing two things: abstaining from fleshly lusts that wage war against the soul, and keeping their behavior excellent among unbelievers by doing good deeds.

Peter knew that God's children used to belong to the world and will therefore be tempted by its allure. "Fleshly lusts" (2:11) refer to all manner of ungodly desires whose appeal lingers on after we're saved. Abstaining from fleshly lusts is necessary and possible for believers in Jesus because we have been called and equipped to exhibit behavior that reflects well on our Father. Although strong temptations "wage war" (v. 11) against us, God's indwelling Spirit enables us to overwhelmingly conquer (Romans 8:37; 1 John 4:4).

However, simply abstaining from evil is not sufficient

to glorify God. Peter says we must also work hard at doing good deeds. That command wasn't something that just popped into his head; it was something Jesus had taught him. Years before, Peter had heard Jesus exhort His disciples to let their light shine in such a way that the people around them would see their good works and glorify God (Matthew 5:16). And he must have remembered that Jesus' command had followed a promise of blessing for those who are persecuted for righteousness sake (Matthew 5:10–12).

Peter's words in these verses reflect those of his Lord. He knew that persecution for righteousness sake often takes the form of slander and that Christians are slandered for any number of reasons. Robert Leighton suggests three that may well encompass all of the others: Christians may bear the brunt of unbelievers' hatred of God because they are available whereas God is not; their behavior may be maligned because it brings unbelievers under distressing conviction; and they may be handy targets for unbelieving attacks against religion in general.[2]

We should not let slander disturb us, however—as long as it is truly slander, and therefore untrue.[3] Righteous conduct will be blessed by God and used as a means of accomplishing all His good pleasure. Peter says that even unbelievers who slander us will, on account of their observance of our good deeds, glorify God in the day of visitation.

Commentators debate about what Peter meant by the phrase "day of visitation" (2:12). Some say he was referring to the "visitation" of God at the final judgment, whereas others believe he was referring to a merciful visitation of gracious salvation. I can't decide, so I'm going to stand with my feet planted firmly in both camps. Since Paul assures us that obedient Christians exude a fragrance of "life to life" and "death to death" among those who are being saved and those who are perishing (2 Corinthians 2:14–16), I will affirm that our good deeds draw some to Christ while establishing an inescapable judgment criterion for those who reject Him.[4]

Abstaining from fleshly lusts and keeping our behavior excellent before unbelievers glorifies God because it fulfills His command to be holy in all our behavior. Scot McKnight helps us understand what it means to be holy in all our behavior when he says,

> We need to realize that holiness is not just a call to read the Bible daily, to pray daily, to be faithful attendees of church, to be tithers, or to follow any other Christian virtues that have become the essence of Christian living. Holiness is a thirst, a drive to know God in his fullness and an unashamed commitment to obey God whatever it costs and wherever we are.[5]

Holy living that glorifies God requires submission to Him— and also to those He has placed in authority.

Freely Submit to Your Rulers
(1 Peter 2:13–17)

Submission is not a popular word in American culture. Most of us born and reared in the USA are addicted to freedom. We are proud of our independence and typically protest the slightest curtailment of our precious liberties. Even following the horrendous attack on our nation on September 11, 2001, many Americans fussed, fumed, and protested when required to submit to "restrictive" security procedures in airports. Surely, they wanted to be "safe and secure" in the air, but apparently did *not* want safety and security to interfere with their freedom of movement. So, if you find yourself bristling at the thought of submission, take comfort in this: Peter is talking about free submission. A contradiction in terms? Not for the Christian!

Peter tells his readers, "Act as free men, and do not use your freedom as a covering for evil, but use it as bondslaves of God" (2:16). His words affirm that we are indeed free in Christ; but freedom in Christ doesn't mean we are free in every sense. It means we are free from the utter futility of trying to earn favor with God (Galatians 5:1–14). It means we are free from our crushing burden of guilt (Galatians 3:13–14). It means we are free from sin's brutal authority over our lives (John 8:31–36; Romans 6:1–23). And it means we are free to serve God with inexpressible joy (Psalm 119:24). But it does *not* mean we are free to do wrong.

Freedom in Christ is freedom to fulfill the purpose for which we were created—to joyfully glorify God during our sojourn as aliens and strangers in this fallen world. God's gracious salvation softened our hard hearts of stone and inclined them toward willing submission to our perfect Father. Our transformation in Christ blessed us with true freedom—the freedom to live in accordance with our design.

However, that freedom, by its very nature, also grants us the ability to eschew submission and live, for a time, in rebellion against God's commands. Ironically, as soon as we do that, we are no longer free. When we use our freedom in Christ as a covering for evil, we shackle ourselves to our old master, who no longer has any authority to direct our behavior (Romans 6:14). And we bring ourselves under the discipline of our heavenly Father, who loves us too much to allow us to persist in such destructive behavior (Hebrews 12:4–11).

As I have grown in my understanding of God's grace, I have gained a sense of great freedom in ministry. As I strengthen my grip on the indicative truth that God's grace cannot be earned or merited in any way, I worry less about whether I am "doing enough" or "doing it right." As I rely on the grace that saved me to also equip me for ministry, I find myself relaxing into more boldness. I hesitate less when confronted with ministry opportunities because I am learning that the power in my obedience comes from God, not from me. I lose less sleep about what I could have done differently because I am growing in my understanding that God will accomplish all His good pleasure, with or without me.

That freedom in ministry is a joyous, liberating, powerful thing. But my human nature tends to abuse it. I'm easily tempted to slack off, take it easy, and not do the hard things. And when I do that, I use my freedom as a covering for evil. When I choose sleep (or TV) over Bible study, ignore opportunities to proclaim the gospel, excuse insensitivity to others' needs with appeals to my busy schedule, or cease striving for excellence in Christian service, I misuse my freedom in Christ. God gives me that freedom to increase my ability to glorify Him, not to make me indifferent to effective service! That's why when I succumb to the temptation to misuse my freedom, He is faithful to discipline me through the convicting work of His Spirit. And He is just as faithful with all of His children.

Peter knew, from his experience, the pain of rebellion and the joy of submission in his relationship with the Father. He knew that God will complete the good work He began by molding us into vessels that display His glory. Peter knew that resistance to God is not only futile but also foolish. He knew that our greatest joys don't result from resisting our Father's design; they result from submitting to His will for our lives.

Therefore, Peter commands his readers, "Submit yourselves for the Lord's sake to every human institution, whether to a king as the one in authority, or to governors as sent by him for the punishment of evildoers and the praise of those who do right. For such is the will of God that by doing right you may silence the ignorance of foolish men" (2:13–15).

The word *submit* means "to place under or to subordinate."[6] It is a relational word typically used in regard to the authority structures God has ordained for His created realm. Contrary to what some folks would like to believe, these authority structures were not the result of the fall of humanity. They were part of God's plan from the beginning. They exist among sinless angels (1 Thessalonians 4:16; Jude 9), the redeemed in heaven (Luke 19:17, 19), and even members of the triune Godhead (1 Corinthians 11:3; 15:28).[7]

God is a God of order, not confusion. And His ordered creation reflects this sparkling facet of His perfect nature. Authority structures in human relationships were ordained by God to accomplish His purposes for His sons and daughters. And we glorify Him when we submit ourselves to them.

Peter talks about authority structures in the government, the marketplace, and the home, and between Christians in general in the verses that follow. His discussion indicates that most of the Christians to whom he was writing were among the "not many mighty, not many noble" about whom Paul speaks in 1 Corinthians 1:26–29. Peter's instructions are addressed, for the most part, to those in positions that require them to submit instead of those to whom others are expected to submit.

First, he tells his readers to submit to the governing authorities. At the time Peter wrote these words, most commentators believe that the cruel and ruthless Emperor Nero was at the helm of Roman government. Christians would not have found it easy or pleasant to submit to him. However, Peter emphasizes that submission is conditioned not on the character of the governing authorities but on the fact that they are set in place by God to maintain order within societies. Even cruel ruthless order is better than anarchy.

Therefore, Christians are to obey the governing authorities unless and until doing so would require them to disobey God. Peter affirms that authority structures themselves have an authority structure that we must observe when they collide with each other. "Honor all people," Peter says, but "love the brotherhood" (2:17). We owe greater devotion to our brothers and sisters in Christ than we do to unbelievers. We must honor all men, unless doing so would prevent us from loving each other (Galatians 5:10).

"Fear God," Peter says, and "honor the king" (2:17). Our reverential esteem for God's majesty takes precedence over submission to human rulers. As long as governmental authorities do not command us to dishonor God, we must honor them. But when the commands of human rulers contradict God's, we must obey God rather than men (Acts 4:19–20; 5:29).

Freely Submit to Your Masters
(1 Peter 2:18–20)

Having dealt with the government, Peter moves to the marketplace. He says,

> Servants, be submissive to your masters with all respect, not only to those who are good and gentle, but also to those who are unreasonable. For this finds favor, if for the sake of conscience toward God a person bears up under sorrows when suffering unjustly. For what credit is there if, when you sin and are harshly treated, you endure it with patience? But if when you do what is right and suffer for it you patiently endure it, this finds favor with God.

The "servants" Peter addresses in these verses were slaves who had no legal rights in the culture. Many of them were professionals (teachers, doctors, musicians) who were treated well, paid wages, and might eventually purchase their freedom. However, they were slaves, which meant their service was involuntary and they were required to submit to masters who were often unjust.

Peter says that believers who find themselves in situations like this should endure harsh treatment with patience because it "finds favor with God" (2:20). Think about that for a moment. If God is a just God (and He is), why would submitting to unjust behavior find favor with Him? Psalms 37 and 73 give us the answer.

We are told not to fret because of evildoers, because God has promised that they will wither like grass (Psalm 37:1–2). Evildoers will be cut off, their arms will be broken, and they will eventually perish (vv. 9, 17, 20). God's children will inherit the land, delight themselves in abundant prosperity, be sustained by the Lord, and rest in His provision of their every need (vv. 11, 17, 22, 23–26).

Although evildoers may prosper, attain positions of power, and oppress the righteous during their time on this earth, they will eventually stand before the Supreme Authority. Then they will be cast down to destruction, destroyed in a moment, and utterly swept away by sudden terrors (Psalm 73:19–20). They will not get away with their evildoing. God's people can rest in the fact that God's justice will triumph. Wayne Grudem summed it up well when he said, "It is the confidence that God will ultimately right all wrongs which enables a Christian to submit to an unjust master without resentment, rebelliousness, self-pity, or despair."[8]

When God's people behave righteously in the midst of harsh treatment, they reflect their reliance on their Father's promises. When they refuse to sin in response to unreasonableness, they display their free submission to God's commands. When they patiently endure the sorrows of this life, they reveal the beauty of their living hope. Such behavior finds favor with God because it glorifies Him.

Notes

1. I. Howard Marshall, *The IVP New Testament Commentary Series: 1 Peter,* ed. Grant R. Osborne (Downers Grove, Ill.: InterVarsity Press, 1991), 77.

2. Robert Leighton and Griffith Thomas, *The Crossway Classic Commentaries: 1 and 2 Peter,* ed. Alister McGrath and J. I. Packer (Wheaton, Ill.: Crossway, 1999), 114.

3. Naturally, we should be bothered when our behavior is maligned with good reason. If unbelievers speak evil of us because our behavior is obnoxious, cruel, insensitive, self-centered, merciless, or unloving, we should take their criticism to heart, repent, and seek their forgiveness.

4. Scot McKnight, in his commentary on 1 Peter, takes the position that the phrase "day of visitation" refers to coming judgment because the normal response of pagans to Christians is not conversion. However, he also affirms the Bible's clear teaching that Christian behavior leads to others' becoming Christians and to a criterion for final judgment. See Scot McKnight, *The NIV Application Commentary: 1 Peter* (Grand Rapids: Zondervan, 1996), 128–29.

5. Ibid., 138.

6. Simon J. Kistemaker, *New Testament Commentary: Exposition of Peter* (Grand Rapids: Baker, 1996), 98.

7. Wayne Grudem, *The Tyndale New Testament Commentaries: 1 Peter* (Grand Rapids: Eerdmans, 1988), 118–19.

8. Ibid., 127.

Exercises

Review

1. Do you think the slogan, "Go Against the Flow," says a mouthful about Christian living? Explain. What are some of the consequences of going against the flow of our culture? How do these consequences help us maintain our distinctiveness as the people of God?

2. Describe the encouragement Peter offers his readers in 1 Peter 2:11–12. (Hint: This encouragement is found in his use of the words "beloved" and "aliens and strangers.")

3. List the two ways Peter says that his readers can throw open doors of testimony and witness as they live as aliens and strangers in their culture. Then describe how obedience to Peter's exhortation (1 Peter 2:11–12) glorifies God.

4. Explain the biblical concept of free submission. Then explain its importance for effective Christian witness.

5. Did authority structures result from the fall? For what reasons did God build authority structures into human relationships? Support your answers with Scripture. List at least four authority structures that Peter discusses in 1 Peter 2:13–3:12. Which of these authority structures affect you personally? List some things that make it difficult for you to submit to authority. List some things that make it easy for you to submit to authority. Does your responsibility to submit to authority depend upon whether it is difficult or easy for you to do so? Support your answer with Scripture.

6. Read Psalms 37 and 73. Record verses that help you understand how patiently enduring unfair harsh treatment finds favor with God.

Application

1. Review your memory verses from the previous lesson. Then begin memorizing one or more of the following:

   Matthew 5:16
   Romans 12:18–21
   Galatians 5:22–25

2. This week use Psalms 37; 73; Matthew 5:11–16; and 2 Corinthians 2:14–16 to help you pray for a renewed commitment to abstaining from fleshly lusts and to keeping your behavior excellent before unbelievers, and for a spirit of free submission to God-ordained authority figures.

3. Have you ever been slandered? (Slander is speaking hurtful, untrue things about someone.) If so, briefly describe how you were slandered. Do you believe you were slandered because you bore the brunt of an unbeliever's hatred for God, you brought someone under distressing conviction, or you were a handy target for an attack against religion in general? If not, describe why you think you were slandered.

   How did you respond to the person who slandered you? Was your response honoring to God? Did your good behavior in that difficult situation cause unbelievers to glorify God? If you answered yes, describe how God received glory and honor from your behavior. Then thank Him for giving you the wisdom and strength to behave as you did. If you answered no, seek forgiveness from your Father in prayer and consider whether you need to ask forgiveness from one or more other people. Then make a plan that will help you keep your behavior excellent before unbelievers when you are slandered in the future. Share your plan with someone who knows you well and loves you enough to hold you accountable to follow through on your plan.

4. Chances are quite good that you are not a slave as some of Peter's first-century readers were. Although you may feel enslaved at times, you do have political rights and freedoms that those readers did not. Does this mean that you can ignore 1 Peter 2:18–20? Explain. Which of your relationships might be comparable to the slave-master relationship of the first century? How will you apply the truths contained in 1 Peter 2:18–20 to those relationships? (Make your application specific by making sure it answers the questions Who? What? When? Where? and How?)

Digging Deeper

1. Kenneth S. Wuest said, "The Christian must always live in the consciousness of the fact that he is being watched by the unsaved, that his responsibility is to bear a clear, ringing, genuine testimony to His God and Savior by the kind of life he lives" (in *Wuest's Word Studies from the Greek New Testament,* vol. 2, *Philippians, Hebrews, The Pastoral Epistles, First Peter, In These Last Days* [Grand Rapids: Eerdmans, 1973], 41).

   Discuss Wuest's statement in light of what you have learned so far in this study.

2. Using good biblical reference books and commentaries, research the phrase "day of visitation" that Peter uses in 1 Peter 2:12. Based on your research, do you believe he is referring to the day of judgment or to a day of gracious salvation? Support your answer with Scripture and careful thinking.

Primary Passage
1 Peter 2:21–3:12

Supplementary Passages
Genesis 18:9–15
Deuteronomy 21:22–23
2 Chronicles 16:9
Psalm 34
Isaiah 52:13–53:12
Matthew 5:43–47; 11:28–30
John 15:18–20; 16:33
Romans 12:9–21
2 Corinthians 5:21
Galatians 5:22–26
Philippians 1:29–2:16
Colossians 3:12–25
1 Thessalonians 3:1–4; 4:9–12
2 Timothy 3:12
Hebrews 12:1–3

Before reading the lesson material, please read the primary Scripture passage listed above and as many of the supplementary passages as time allows. Then briefly summarize in your notebook what you have read. (Do not go into detail. Limit your summary to a brief description of the people, events, and/or ideas discussed in the passages.)

6

The Appeal of Free Submission (2)

*If we really understand what being a Christian means—
that this Christ, the living God, actually comes in to rule
one's life—then everything must change: values, goals,
priorities, desires, and habits.*   —Charles Colson

On my first day of ninth grade, a girl I didn't recognize greeted me in the hallway like we were old friends. "Who was that?" I asked the girl walking with me. She told me, and I dropped my brand-new zipper notebook on the toe of my shiny new loafers.

The girl who had greeted me like we were old friends *was* an old friend, albeit one I hadn't seen since school ended in May. At that time she had been about my height (short), at least twenty pounds overweight, and completely unskilled in the womanly arts of arranging hair, applying makeup, and selecting clothing. But on the first day of ninth grade, she was three inches taller, quite slender, and definitely pulled together. My old friend had been completely transformed in the space of one summer.

I was so intrigued, I sat with her at lunch to find out what happened. She explained that a natural growth spurt coupled with an eight-week modeling course had made the difference. As I talked with her, I realized that the difference went deeper than her appearance. Not only was she better looking, she was also more poised, more confident, more mature, and more worldly-wise.

As you might have guessed, my friend's stunning metamorphosis changed her life drastically. Those of us who had hung out with her in the eighth grade, being still too gawky and giggly to feel comfortable with her, began to avoid her. And the "in" crowd she had always admired began seeking her out. She quickly realized what being beautiful, poised, confident, mature, and worldly-wise meant: She had what it took to be wildly popular. And she proceeded to hand popularity the reins of her life. By the end of ninth grade, everything about her had changed— her values, her goals, her priorities, her desires, and her habits. Unfortunately, few of the changes were good.

My old friend's sad example stands in stark contrast to the stunning metamorphosis experienced by Christians. That's because our metamorphosis isn't something we do to ourselves so that we can accomplish some personal goal. Rather, it is something that God does for us so that we can accomplish His purposes for us.

God, in His mercy and grace, chose us in eternity past to receive salvation through the atoning work of His Son, Jesus Christ. Then He extended His mercy and grace by equipping us, through the work of His Holy Spirit, to joyfully glorify Him in our obedience (Ephesians 1:3–14). God's grace working in us allows Him to work through us.

Peter's perspective on Christian living emphasizes the fact that conversion transforms us for a purpose. God not only chose us (1 Peter 1:2), "caused us to be born again" (v. 3), and guaranteed our inheritance (vv. 4–5). He also "called [us] out of darkness into His marvelous light" (2:9) to patiently endure unjust suffering (v. 21), to bless and be blessed (3:9), and to enjoy eternal glory with Christ (5:10). The living stones God selects for His spiritual house are chosen, designed, and equipped to offer up spiritual sacrifices acceptable to God through Jesus Christ (2:5). We are to be holy in all our behavior so that we will reflect our Father's glory.

As Charles Colson has well stated, being a Christian means coming under authority. It means "placing ourselves under or subordinating ourselves" to the absolute rule of our Lord Jesus Christ. It means that everything about us changes as God's indwelling Spirit graciously changes our hearts. He graciously gives us new values, new goals, new priorities, and new desires. And He graciously helps us develop new habits of righteousness behavior. God's grace is the means by which we freely submit to His Son.[1]

We are in the middle of a long section of verses in which Peter exhorts his readers to keep their behavior excellent before unbelievers so that God will be glorified. He tells us to do this by patterning our lives after the example of Christ as we freely submit to our rulers, our masters, our spouses, and each other in general.

The Perfect Pattern of Free Submission
(1 Peter 2:21–25)

Peter's words to suffering first-century saints scattered throughout Pontus, Galatia, Cappadocia, Asia, and Bithynia bear the indelible marks of scriptural timelessness. His apostolic instruction, supersaturated with hope and encouragement for those folks at that time, comfort us now just as much as it did them then. The ways and means by which Christians suffer certainly change with the times, but God's purpose for suffering has not changed a bit. Peter tells us that suffering is inexorably linked with Christian living for a very good reason. It conforms us to the image of our Lord Jesus Christ and thus equips us to live distinctly enough to glorify God.

The distinctive living that glorifies God sets us apart from the sinful ways of this world. It requires us to go against the flow of unredeemed human industry. It demands that we swim against the current in a sea of lost sinners. Living like that sets us up as beacons and targets. Christian distinctiveness attracts those who are being called to salvation by God's Holy Spirit. And at the same time, it incites those still in darkness toward abusive behavior. That fact hasn't changed down through the centuries. And neither has our need to depend on God's gracious enabling to glorify Him in our distinctiveness.

The desire and the ability to live distinctively are given to us as free gifts of God's grace when we are regenerated. Our hard hearts of stone are made soft and responsive to God's purposes for us (Ezekiel 11:17–20; 36:23–27). And our bondage to sin's authority is broken when we are made slaves of God (Romans 6:1–7, 14, 22). However, desire and ability, all by themselves, won't make us distinctive. That's because other people can't see our desire and ability. What they see is our obedience to God's commands. Thus, it is our obedience, quickened by God's gracious gifts of desire and ability, that glorifies Him.

That's why Peter's letter is chocked full of imperatives—and why those imperatives are grounded in indicative truth. The facts of what God has done for us and in us equip and motivate us to obey His commands. Peter knew that his readers would not find it easy to freely submit to cruel and abusive authority. So right in the middle of Peter's difficult call to submit to authority, he pauses to encourage God's people to draw their hope from Jesus Christ's perfect pattern of free submission.

For you have been called for this purpose, since Christ also suffered for you, leaving you an example for you to follow in His steps, who committed no sin, nor was any deceit found in His mouth; and while being reviled, He did not revile in return; while suffering, He uttered no threats, but kept entrusting Himself to Him who judges righteously; and He Himself bore our sins in His body on the cross, so that we might die to sin and live to righteousness; for by His wounds you were healed. For you were continually straying like sheep, but now you have returned to the Shepherd and Guardian of your souls. (1 Peter 2:21–25)

Peter was speaking from personal remembrance. He had watched Jesus suffer unjustly at the hands of cruel, abusive authority figures. He had seen his Master freely submit to unbelievers who reviled Him, beat Him, and eventually killed Him. And he had heard Jesus refrain from responding in kind or uttering threats. I'm sure that as Peter observed the events of his Lord's trial, conviction, and death, he did not understand why Jesus suffered in silence.

After all, Peter was the man who had resorted to violence in defense of his leader. Peter knew Jesus Christ was God in the flesh. He could have called more than twelve legions of angels to His defense (Matthew 26:53). And as Peter watched Jesus suffer unjustly, he may well have wondered why Jesus didn't call them.

Years later when he wrote the epistles we're studying, Peter did understand. And with a little help from Isaiah's prophecy regarding God's suffering Servant (Isaiah 52:13–53:12), he gives us an excellent threefold explanation.

Jesus trusted God, knowing that He judges righteously. Jesus knew that the authority of human rulers comes from

God, that they will eventually answer to Him, and that His perfect justice will ultimately triumph (Psalms 37; 73; John 19:10–11).

Jesus recognized that His suffering was purposeful. He had come to earth to atone for the sins of God's elect, an act that meant paying the wages of sin on their behalf. The joy of accomplishing redemption for God's chosen people made His suffering worthwhile (Hebrews 12:2).

Jesus, as the Shepherd and Guardian of the souls of all believers, not only patterned the lifestyle of obedience to which we have been called. He also assured us that we are able to live out that calling. By His wounds we were healed. We are no longer in bondage to sin because we are in union with Him. In His death and resurrection, we died to sin and rose to live righteously (Romans 6:1–14).

The author of Hebrews echoes Peter's hope-filled description of Jesus' perfect pattern of free submission. He exhorts us to "run with endurance the race that is set before us, fixing our eyes on Jesus, the author and perfecter of faith, who for the joy set before Him endured the cross, despising the shame, and has sat down at the right hand of the throne of God. For consider Him who has endured such hostility by sinners against Himself, so that you may not grow weary and lose heart" (Hebrews 12:1–3).

Jesus Christ's free submission to cruel, abusive authority figures reflected His free submission to the will of the Father. As such, it directs and encourages us in our efforts to keep our behavior excellent before unbelievers so that God will be glorified. Free submission to those God has placed in authority over us reflects our trust in Him, our confidence in His purposes, and our transformed dependence on His gracious enabling.

After this pause that refreshes, Peter returned to his exhortation. He has already commanded us to glorify God by freely submitting to our rulers and masters. Now he tells us to glorify God through free submission in our homes and in all our relationships.

Freely Submit in the Home
(1 Peter 3:1–7)

First-century Christians understood that in Christ there is neither Jew nor Greek, slave nor free man, male nor female. Therefore, they didn't limit their preaching to Jews, free men, and males. They preached the gospel to all, and as a result many Greeks, slaves, and women came to faith in Christ Jesus. Newly saved Greeks did not necessarily find themselves embroiled in sticky relational problems because of their conversion, but slaves and women frequently did.

At that time in history, households routinely accepted and practiced the religious beliefs adopted by the master, husband, and father. No one expected or encouraged slaves and women to adopt a different religion—no one except Christians, that is. Christianity elevated commitment to God above all human authority and rightly taught that salvation in Christ required ultimate devotion to the one true God. When redeemed slaves and women disavowed the religious beliefs of their masters and husbands, their actions were often construed as rebellion against established authority.

Peter recognized that slaves and women were acutely vulnerable to abusive treatment and would therefore be sorely tempted to keep their Christianity quiet. So he singled them out for specific instruction. Slaves were to bear witness to their faith in Christ, not only in words but also by being submissive to their masters "with all respect" regardless of how they were treated. For the sake of conscience toward God, they were to find favor with Him by keeping their behavior excellent before unbelievers. And now Peter says that Christian women married to unbelievers were to bear witness to their faith "in the same way."

Peter said,

> You wives, be submissive to your own husbands so
> that even if any of them are disobedient to the word,
> they may be won without a word by the behavior
> of their wives, as they observe your chaste and re-
> spectful behavior. Your adornment must not be
> merely external—braiding the hair, and wearing gold
> jewelry, or putting on dresses; but let it be the hid-
> den person of the heart, with the imperishable qual-
> ity of a gentle and quiet spirit, which is precious in
> the sight of God. For in this way in former times the
> holy women also, who hoped in God, used to adorn
> themselves, being submissive to their own husbands;
> just as Sarah obeyed Abraham, calling him lord, and
> you have become her children if you do what is right
> without being frightened by any fear. (3:1–6)

The first thing we should notice about Peter's words to
the wives is that they do not contain a sure-fire procedure
for saving pagan husbands. I have known women who have
faithfully lived out these instructions before unsaved husbands right up to the day those husbands stepped into a
godless eternity. Without regeneration by God's Holy Spirit,
no amount of chaste and respectful behavior will convert
a lost husband. Peter affirms that when he says that husbands *may* be won as they observe the behavior of believing wives. Peter's primary concern here is that the wife's
behavior glorify God, whether or not God's Spirit works in
her husband to bring him to salvation.

The second thing we should notice about Peter's words
to the wives is that they do not forbid them to speak to
their husbands about the gospel. Faith comes by hearing
the word of Christ (Romans 10:17); therefore, wives should
not refrain absolutely from sharing the gospel with un-

saved husbands. However, they should avoid unnecessary friction and tension by whispering truth with their mouths while letting their lives shout its veracity. A lost husband who sees Christ's love displayed in his wife's behavior will be more likely to view the salvation message as credible. That's why Peter goes on to say that Christian wives should be more obsessed with their character than they are with their looks.

Bible commentator and historian J. N. D. Kelly affirms that the Word "must of course be the converting instrument, but in certain cases the eloquent silence of Christian deportment is its most effective vehicle."[2] And I. Howard Marshall points out that these wives were most likely living with men who had already heard and rejected the gospel. Therefore, their sermons should be short on words and long on submission, good character, and freedom from fear.[3]

The third thing we should notice about Peter's words to the wives is that they emphasize trusting God in distress just as did Peter's words to those in submission to rulers and masters. The gentle and quiet spirit, which is precious in the sight of God because it reflects calm dependence on Him, is not uniquely feminine. Jesus Christ had such a spirit (Matthew 11:29), and Paul encouraged all Christians to cultivate it (1 Thessalonians 4:11–12). A gentle and quiet spirit is a non-gender-specific fruit of the Spirit that grows sweet and flavorful in the fertile soil of complete trust in God's goodness, mercy, and grace.

Christian wives who submit to their unsaved husbands while entrusting themselves to Him who judges righteously will not be frightened by any fear. They will keep their behavior excellent before unbelievers so that God will be glorified. And they will manifest a sweet aroma of the knowledge of Him among those who are being saved and those who are perishing.

A close friend of mine is married to an unbeliever. She

loves him and intensely desires his salvation. But she loves God more than she loves her husband and understands that He alone can breathe life into a dead heart.

The thing I admire most about my friend is the way she lives out what she says she believes. She has not shouldered responsibility for saving her husband. She knows that is not her burden to bear. She has learned from God's Word that she has been called to glorify God in all circumstances of life. So she freely speaks of her faith to her husband—while seeking to reflect the fruit of the Spirit in her words and her actions. She works hard at loving her husband by applying 1 Corinthians 13:4–8a in their relationship. She radiates joy and, as far as it depends on her, seeks peace in her marriage. She is patient and kind, even when her husband is not.

She does what is good and stands firm in her faith, trusting in God to work out His purposes (whatever they may be) through her obedience. She maintains a gentle demeanor by exercising self-control in the power of the Spirit. Her life is worthy of emulation because it glorifies God while creating the best possible atmosphere in which God may be pleased to call her husband to repentance and faith.

Christian wives are not the only family members Peter admonishes to bear witness of their faith through free submission. He also calls Christian husbands to testify of their trust in God by freely submitting to His ordained purpose for their authority. Peter tells them, "You husbands in the same way, live with your wives in an understanding way, as with someone weaker [in some translations, a weaker vessel],[4] since she is a woman; and show her honor as a fellow heir of the grace of life, so that your prayers will not be hindered" (3:7).[5]

The authority bestowed upon Christian husbands must never to be used to oppress or belittle their wives. Rather, it should be exercised wisely and lovingly so as to reflect to the world the husband's desire to nurture, protect, and cherish his wife in their common pursuit of God's kingdom and righteousness.

Freely Submit to One Another
(1 Peter 3:8–12)

Peter summarizes his exhortation to Christians to keep their behavior excellent before unbelievers with a call to freely submit to one another in love:

> To sum up, all of you be harmonious, sympathetic, brotherly, kindhearted, and humble in spirit; not returning evil for evil, or insult for insult, but giving a blessing instead; for you were called for the very purpose that you might inherit a blessing. For
>
> > "The one who desires life, to love and see good days,
> > Must keep his tongue from evil and his lips from speaking deceit.
> > He must turn away from evil and do good;
> > He must seek peace and pursue it.
> > For the eyes of the Lord are toward the righteous,
> > And His ears attend to their prayer,
> > But the face of the Lord is against those who do evil."

The word *brotherly* in verse 8 is a translation of the Greek word *philadelphos,* which refers to the deep affectionate love between brothers and sisters. Perhaps Peter places it in the center of the Christian relational qualities he mentions since it produces and is in turn intensified by the others. Brotherly loves fosters harmony of belief and purpose, sympathetic concern for each other's needs, compassionate activity to meet those needs, and humble self-sacrifice in the church's common pursuit of God's kingdom and righteousness. And the more Christians freely submit to one another in each of these four ways, the deeper their love for each other grows.

Peter reminds his readers that they are free to bless others who persecute them because they are secure in their knowledge of what God has done for them and in them. They are living stones in God's spiritual house, unshakably built on the solid foundation of the Living Stone, Jesus Christ. They have been called to proclaim the excellencies of their Master Builder in all circumstances of life and to inherit the blessing of eternal glory with Christ. Nothing devised by the world, the flesh, or the devil can defile, diminish, or destroy their inheritance or prevent them from receiving it. God's indomitable power and unquenchable love preserve it and protect them.

Christians are therefore free to submit to each other in love and to return blessing for cursing. In so doing, we live out God's purposes for us by keeping our behavior excellent before unbelievers so that they, on account of our good deeds, will glorify God in the day of visitation. Peter encourages us with assurance from Psalm 34 that such behavior finds favor with God, will eventually be vindicated in perfect justice, and is the secret of loving life and seeing good days here on this earth.

We were created and saved to glorify God. Thus, we find our deepest joys in pursuit of the obedience that reflects well on Him. If I may be so bold as to expand some wise words of John Piper's: God is most glorified in us when we are most joyous in our pursuit of His kingdom and righteousness.[6]

Notes

1. For deeper insights into this intriguing truth, I recommend Jerry Bridges, *Transforming Grace: Living Confi-*

dently in God's Unfailing Love (Colorado Springs: Nav-Press, 1991); Jerry Bridges, *The Discipline of Grace: God's Role and Our Role in the Pursuit of Holiness* (Colorado Springs: NavPress, 1994); and Bryan Chapell, *Holiness by Grace: Delighting in the Joy That Is Our Strength* (Wheaton, Ill.: Crossway, 2001).

2. J. N. D. Kelly, *Black's New Testament Commentaries: The Epistles of Peter and Jude,* ed. Henry Chadwick (London: A&C Black, 1969; Peabody, Mass.: Hendrickson, 1969), 128. (By the way, if you are unfamiliar with Kelly's old-fashioned word *deportment,* look it up!)

3. I. Howard Marshall, *The IVP New Testament Commentary Series: 1 Peter,* ed. Grant R. Osborne (Downers Grove, Ill.: InterVarsity Press, 1991), 98.

4. For an excellent treatment of the phrase "weaker vessel" (v. 7, NASB 1977) see Stuart Scott, *The Exemplary Husband: A Biblical Perspective* (Bemidji, Minn.: Focus Publishing, 2000).

5. Peter seems to assume that believing husbands will have believing wives. His assumption may be related to the cultural phenomenon we mentioned that created difficulty for slaves and wives. When a man converted to Christianity, his entire household was expected to convert with him. Although Peter does not address the husband's evangelistic responsibilities in this letter, we can assume that one of a newly converted Christian man's highest priorities would be determining whether his household was truly converted. Peter's assumption that believing husbands will have believing wives may indicate that these men were responsibly pursuing evangelism within their households.

6. John Piper is well known for this delightful revision of the Westminster Shorter Catechism's answer to its first question: "God is most glorified in us when we are most satisfied in Him."

Exercises

Review

1. Relate Charles Colson's words that introduce this chapter to the stunning metamorphosis experienced by Christians at the time they are redeemed and converted.

2. Describe the inexorable link between Christian living and suffering. Then explain the necessity of obedience in Christian living.

3. Read Isaiah 52:13–53:12 and 1 Peter 2:21–25. Describe Jesus' perfect pattern of free submission. In what specific ways are we to pattern our behavior after His example? Which aspects of this pattern are particularly convicting and encouraging for you?

4. Do you think that 1 Peter 2:21–25 is accurately described as a pause that refreshes? Explain your answer.

5. What sticky relational problems might newly converted slaves and women have encountered at the time Peter wrote his first epistle? How does Peter exhort them to deal with these problems? Are his exhortations relevant in the twenty-first century? Explain your answer.

6. Discuss at least three significant things we should notice in Peter's words to wives.

7. Does Peter forbid Christian women to wear braids, gold jewelry, and dresses? Explain 1 Peter 3:3 in light of its immediate context, 1 Peter 2:11–3:12.

8. Read Genesis 18:9–15. Based on this passage, discuss possible reasons why Peter referred to Sarah's obedience to Abraham in 1 Peter 3:6.

9. Explain the connection between the relational qualities Peter mentions in 1 Peter 3:8.

10. Read Psalm 34 and 1 Peter 3:8–12. Then use the truths contained in these passages to describe the freedom of Christians to submit to one another in love and to return blessing for cursing.

Application

1. Review your memory verses from the previous lesson. Then begin memorizing one or more of the following:

   Isaiah 52:13–53:12 (If you choose to memorize this passage, consider yourself excused from further memory work.)
   Philippians 2:14–16
   1 Peter 3:8–9

2. This week, use Isaiah 52:13–53:12 and 1 Peter 2:11–3:12 in your prayer time to help you praise God for what He has done for you and in you through Jesus Christ; thank Him for His gracious gifts of desire and ability to do His will; confess your sins of not making use of His gracious gifts; and renew your commitment to keeping your behavior excellent before unbelievers so that God will be glorified.

3. Study Isaiah 52:13–53:12; Hebrews 12:1–3; and 1 Peter 2:21–25. Describe the similarities you see in these passages. According to these passages, what has Christ done for you if you are a believer? What does Christ's attitude and behavior in these passages teach you about suffering? Based on these passages, how can you endure suffering at the hands of unjust authority figures without losing hope? List one or more examples of suffering that you are experiencing now as a result of being in a position of submission. Describe your attitude and behavior in this situation before you studied this lesson. Has what you learned in this lesson revealed any changes that you need to make in your attitude or behavior in regard to this situation? If so, explain. Has what you learned in this lesson encouraged you in this situation? If so, explain.

4. Consult a standard dictionary (and a Greek dictionary if you have one) and write out definitions of the following words:

> harmonious (*homophrōn*):
> sympathetic (*sympathēs*):
> brotherly (*philadelphos*):
> kindhearted (*eusplanchnos*):
> humble (*tapeinophrōn*):

Now think about your behavior during the past several weeks. List several examples of how you have displayed each of these characteristics in your relationships with other people. Based on your list, which of these characteristics appear to be difficult for you to display? Read and meditate on Hebrews 4:12–13. Then examine your heart (enlist a mature Christian to help you if necessary) to determine the source of your difficulty.

Are you harboring resentment, hatred, or bitterness? Are you struggling with anger, fear, or worry? Are you succumbing to self-centeredness, arrogance, or pride? Are you nursing a grudge or licking wounds resulting from perceived unfair treatment? Once you have determined the source of your difficulty, make a specific, step-by-step plan that will help you kill the root of the problem so you can begin to reflect all of these qualities in your relationships with others.

5. Do you customarily return blessing for cursing? List specific examples of your recent behavior to support your answer. Study Psalm 34; James 3:1–12; and 1 Peter 3:8–12. Use these verses to help you make a plan that will help you develop the habit of returning blessing for cursing. (Your plan should include specific steps that alert you to temptations, refer you to relevant Scripture passages, remind you to pray, suggest specific courses of behavior, and help you rejoice when you succeed in returning blessing for cursing—and help you repent and seek forgiveness when you fail to do so.)

Digging Deeper

1. In his commentary on 1 Peter, Peter H. Davids says that Peter's concern in this part of his letter is not so much life within the Christian community but life at those points where the Christian community interfaces with the world around it (*The New International Commentary on the New Testament: The First Epistle of Peter,* ed. Ned B. Stonehouse, F. F. Bruce, and Gordon D. Fee [Grand Rapids: Eerdmans, 1990], 115). Scot McKnight in his commentary makes a similar point when he says, "The exhortation to submit . . . is part of a larger pattern: living a holy life before unbelievers with the hope that

such conduct will have a positive impact on them" (*The NIV Application Commentary: 1 Peter* [Grand Rapids: Zondervan, 1996], 181).

Reread 1 Peter 2:11–3:12 in light of these insightful comments and summarize Peter's main points regarding how Christians should live in the world. Then describe how the timeless principles Peter teaches in this section of Scripture are as relevant today as they were in the first century.

Primary Passage
1 Peter 3:13–4:6

Supplementary Passages
Genesis 6:1–9:17
Psalms 56; 62:5–8; 110:1–2; 119:116
Proverbs 15:1–3
Isaiah 8:11–13
Matthew 5:10–12
John 15:18–20; 16:33
Acts 2:22–36
Romans 8:31
2 Corinthians 2:14–16; 5:21
Galatians 2:11–21
Ephesians 5:1–10; 6:10–20
Colossians 2:8–15; 4:6
2 Timothy 1:12
Hebrews 9:27–28
1 Peter 2:11–12, 19–20

Before reading the lesson material, please read the primary Scripture passage listed above and as many of the supplementary passages as time allows. Then briefly summarize in your notebook what you have read. (Do not go into detail. Limit your summary to a brief description of the people, events, and/or ideas discussed in the passages.)

7

The Power of a
Humble Witness

*Since hope already anticipates the blessings that will be
experienced at the revelation of Christ, it enables believers to live in accordance with those values rather
than in accordance with the values . . . of the culture
around them. Hope . . . is critical to living properly.*
— Peter H. Davids

W hat comes into your mind when you hear the word
humble? If I were to tell you that my friend Joan[1] is the most
humble person on the face of the earth, how would you
picture her? Soft-spoken and unassertive? Shy and retir-
ing? Someone who sits on the back row and rarely, if ever,
opens her mouth? Someone who is lacking in confidence
and a far cry from bold?

If that's how you would picture my humble friend Joan,
you'd be completely wrong about her. Joan's gentle and
quiet spirit is outspoken and confident, bold and coura-
geous. She's not shy about bearing witness to her living
hope. So what makes her so humble? Her complete de-

pendence on God's gracious enabling. She is "so humble" because she eschews self-confidence in favor of Christ-confidence.

My friend Joan understands what it means to die to self and live to Christ. She knows she is inadequate in herself to work out her salvation. But she also knows that God works in her to equip her for every good deed. She stands firm in the Lord and in the strength of His might.

Contrary to what some folks seem to think, true humility is not characterized by downcast eyes, shuffling feet, and self-consciously muttering, "Oh dear, I could never do that." True humility fixes its eyes on Jesus Christ, stands firm on God's truth, and proclaims, "I can do all things through Him who strengthens me" (Phil. 4:13). True humility's witness is undeniably powerful because it displays and proclaims the living hope of salvation.

Humility's Power Is Living Hope
(1 Peter 3:13–17)

The undeniable power of humble witness flows irresistibly from Peter's perspective on Christian living. Those who stand firm and grow in the true grace of God know they don't stand alone against opposition. God's Word has taught them that they stand united with Christ who has already won the ultimate victory. Their living hope in their sure inheritance sets their hearts and minds on eternity instead of this world. And it gives them great boldness in the proclamation of truth. As they humbly rely on God's grace to fuel confident testimony, their powerful impact cannot be denied.

However, Peter's perspective on Christian living does not come equipped with a cruise-control setting. It requires constant vigilance and active effort on our part. All redeemed saints of God must work hard at maintaining their eternal perspectives. No one is immune to the danger of shifting his or her focus to the things of this world. Even Peter, as a mature saint of God and respected church leader, lost his perspective at one point, caved in to the pressure of opposition, and weakened his witness.

The apostle Paul tells us in Galatians 2:11–21 that he "opposed [Peter] to his face, because . . . he began to withdraw and hold himself aloof [from the Gentiles], fearing the party of the circumcision." Peter stumbled badly over a fear of man, and God used his brother Paul to restore his perspective. Perhaps the memory of his failure and the lesson it taught him spurred him to write this exhortation to first-century Christians whose difficult circumstances had heightened their vulnerability to the same temptation.

> Who is there to harm you if you prove zealous for what is good? But even if you should suffer for the sake of righteousness, you are blessed. And do not fear their intimidation, and do not be troubled, but sanctify Christ as Lord in your hearts, always being ready to make a defense to everyone who asks you to give an account for the hope that is in you, yet with gentleness and reverence; and keep a good conscience so that in the thing in which you are slandered, those who revile your good behavior in Christ may be put to shame. For it is better, if God should will it so, that you suffer for doing what is right rather than for doing what is wrong. (1 Peter 3:13–17)

These words follow Peter's assurance from Psalm 34 that "the eyes of the Lord are toward the righteous, and His ears attend to their prayer, but the face of the Lord is against those who do evil" (v. 12). Thus they serve to encourage his readers not to fall prey to the fear of man. Peter reminds us that even if unbelievers oppose our righteous behavior, we are blessed. We are God's children, His heirs, safe in His care. Therefore, we should not think of blessing in terms of the absence of suffering but rather in terms of our standing with God. We are blessed in our privileged right to serve God in the strength of humility by wisely relying on His unfailing promises.

Peter knew, from his failure, that even mature believers are tempted to fear man. That's because none of us like to suffer. Hostile abuse has a way of wrenching our focus away from "the heavenlies" to our immediate circumstances. Being physically or emotionally hurt entices us to exchange Peter's perspective on Christian living for a self-centered one. And whenever we slip into shortsighted self-centeredness, we're apt to fall prey to the fear of man and miss opportunities for humble witness.

Therefore, if we want our lives to display the undeniable power that glorifies God, we must work hard at maintaining a long-sighted, God-centered perspective. But how do we do that? Edmund Clowney gives us a good answer: "Both the boldness and the humility needed for witness come about through a fundamental exchange. Christians must exchange the fear of men for the fear of the Lord."[2] The "fundamental exchange" he refers to is illustrated in Peter's use of a quotation from Isaiah 8:12–13. He takes an Old Testament passage referring to God (1 Peter 3:14b) and applies it to Christ (v. 15), setting fear of God equal with "sanctify[ing] Christ as Lord in our hearts."

Sanctifying Christ as Lord in our hearts acknowledges Him as the sovereign Lord of the universe. It sets our minds and our hearts on His providential control of every circumstance of our lives. And it reminds us not only of His irresistible power but also of His loving care of His own. It extends our vision beyond our immediate difficulties to our eternal inheritance. And it causes us to delight in a hope inexpressibly greater than avoidance of suffering. Sanctifying Christ as Lord in our hearts fixes our eyes on the joy set before us and thereby breaks fear-of-man's grip on our behavior.

On September 10, 2001, I boarded an airplane in Albuquerque and flew to Fort Lauderdale, Florida. The next morning, while I was speaking to a women's Bible study group, terrorists launched a hideous and shocking attack on our nation. Later that afternoon as I watched the attack replayed on television, I found myself at a clearly marked ministry crossroad. Would I continue getting on airplanes to travel and speak about God's truth? Or would I "ground myself" as I had done years before when I experienced another dramatic airplane scare? Would I fear man and succumb to shortsighted, self-centered self-protectiveness? Or would I fear God, trust His merciful grace, hang on tight to His promises, and continue to do what He had called me to do?

I praise God that the decision was not hard to make. Following my earlier vow "never to fly again," I had learned from God's Word that my position in Christ is a much greater blessing than avoidance of suffering. God then faithfully "forced" me to put what I'd learned into practice. He called me to a ministry that necessitated getting on airplanes. For more than five years I boarded airplanes obediently—but in fear and trembling. I trusted God enough to obey Him, but not enough to relax. My fear of God was waging a vicious war with my fear of harm.

On September 11, 2001, the war suddenly ended. As I watched the replays of the attack, God blessed me with an amazing awareness of His absolute, indisputable, and invincible sovereignty. Although He did not author the evil perpetrated that day, He controlled it completely. God wasn't surprised by the events of that morning. The forces of evil didn't catch Him off guard. What the terrorists intended for evil, God intended for good.

That amazing awareness of God's sovereign control over something that evil filled me with an astounding sense of utter security. I knew (for a fact, without doubt) that no one died accidentally on September 11, 2001. Every one of God's children was completely safe in His care on that morning. Those who had not been appointed to die at that time "just happened" to be somewhere else. And those who had been appointed to die at that time received the grace they needed to do so to His glory.

My fear of flying crumbled right along with the TV images of the Twin Towers. Close friends and family (who had been speculating I'd never get on an airplane again!) were pop-eyed in surprise when they heard that I not only boarded a flight five days later but actually fell asleep on the leg between Fort Lauderdale and Dallas. Finally, I trusted God enough to relax. Fear-of-man's grip on my behavior had been broken—at least in regard to getting on airplanes.

Interestingly, I immediately found myself "swimming upstream to the beat of a different drummer." I have yet to discover anyone else who *lost* his or her fear of flying on September 11, 2001! The distinctiveness of "the hope that I have" has generated a wide range of reactions. Some folks have questioned me with peaked curiosity, some have attacked with active hostility, and others have responded with Spirit-led seeking.

Peter exhorts us to be prepared to answer those who react to our living hope. Stop and think about that for a minute or two. How do you prepare for an upcoming trip, a presentation at work, or next week's exam? You prepare beforehand by acquiring knowledge, making plans, and ordering your frame of mind and emotions. Preparation equips you to effectively handle anticipated events.

In much the same way, preparing to give an account for the hope in us occurs before we are questioned, not on the spur of the moment.[3] Since we don't always know when we will be questioned, effective preparation entails regular study of Scripture, continual prayer for guidance and strength, and habitual reliance on God's indwelling Spirit. Consistent involvement in those pursuits cultivates the long-sighted, God-centered perspective that dispels fear of man and spawns humble witness.

Since humble witness sanctifies Christ as Lord, it never speaks self-defensively but instead responds gently to questioners and with reverence toward God. It flows out of a believer's clear conscience and puts to shame those who slander our good behavior in Christ. It stands firmly dependent on God's gracious enabling and willingly suffers for doing what's right. It exudes a power that cannot be denied because its living hope springs from the triumph of Christ.

The Sure Basis of Christian Confidence
(1 Peter 3:18–22)

The confidence that empowers truly humble witness is rooted and grounded in the atonement of Christ. Understanding the indicative truth of what Christ has done for us and in us equips us to obey God's imperatives to testify boldly. When we face suffering at the hands of unbelievers, we do well to remember that the best they can do is win a few skirmishes. They cannot win the war because Jesus Christ has already triumphed over the forces of evil. Peter reminds Christians under attack for their faith to stand firm and grow strong in the fact and the result of God's gracious salvation:

> For Christ also died for sins once for all, the just for the unjust, so that He might bring us to God, having been put to death in the flesh, but made alive in the spirit; in which also He went and made proclamation to the spirits now in prison, who once were disobedient, when the patience of God kept waiting in the days of Noah, during the construction of

> the ark, in which a few, that is, eight persons, were brought safely through the water. Corresponding to that, baptism now saves you—not the removal of dirt from the flesh, but an appeal to God for a good conscience—through the resurrection of Jesus Christ, who is at the right hand of God, having gone into heaven, after angels and authorities and powers had been subjected to Him.

Peter's words are, without doubt, some of the most challenging in all of Scripture to interpret. Commentators disagree about where Jesus went after He was "made alive in the spirit" (v. 18), what He proclaimed to "spirits now in prison" (v. 19) and who those spirits were "who were once disobedient" (v. 20).[4] They also disagree about the significance of the reference to Noah and the ark. But after diverging to spill gallons of ink over reams of paper chasing down numerous possible meanings for what Peter said, they seem to converge in general agreement on the main point of the passage.

All of the commentators I read came to the conclusion that Peter intended his words to encourage his readers to fearlessly face opposition. Most of them emphasized that Peter encouraged his readers by pointing them to the fact that their salvation unites them with Christ who has decisively triumphed over the powers of evil. The result of that fact is that they should not be intimidated by their opponents.

When Christ died for sins once for all, He uniquely, finally, and for all time, secured God's forgiveness for His chosen children. When He was put to death in the flesh and made alive in the spirit, He defeated sin's power to separate us from God and empowered us to live for His glory. And when He arose and ascended to the right hand of God, He proclaimed His decisive victory over the powers of evil and subjected all created beings to His undisputed authority.

When we are baptized into Christ Jesus, we are united with Him in His death and resurrection. His victory is our victory and becomes our security as we walk through this world. Just as those eight souls in the ark had nothing to fear from the rising flood waters, we have nothing to fear from the world's opposition. We can face persecution, hostility, and daily harassment confident in the knowledge that we will receive our inheritance. Although the water of baptism has no power in itself to save us, it pictures the faith in Christ Jesus that does have that power. Baptism testifies to the fact that God's chosen children are safe in His care.

Although much of this passage is clear as mud to most students of Scripture, Peter's penchant for practical-minded theology shines through clear as crystal. When he describes Jesus Christ's suffering and ultimate vindication, he puts in the hands of embattled believers the tried and true weapons of hope and encouragement. Because our salvation unites us with Christ, His indisputable triumph assures us of victory. Humble dependence on the fact and result of God's gracious salvation emboldens our testimony in all manner of circumstances.

The Triumph of Christ Doesn't Allow Us to Coast
(1 Peter 4:1–6)

Peter seems to have sensed that a few of his readers might misconstrue his assurance of ultimate victory and think they are free to sit back, relax, and coast into heaven. So he quickly slams the door shut on that line of thinking. "Therefore," he exhorts us, "since Christ has suffered in the flesh, arm yourselves also with the same purpose, because he who has suffered in the flesh has ceased from sin, so as to live the rest of the time in the flesh no longer for the lusts of men, but for the will of God" (vv. 1–2).

In other words, this is no time to shift into neutral. Although Christ has indeed triumphed and the ultimate victory is most assuredly ours, the war is not over. God's enemy Satan has not surrendered. We can expect ongoing assaults from the world, the flesh, and the devil for as long as we live. If you've studied history, you may recall that wars seldom stop at the moment one side is surely defeated. Defeated foes have a way of fighting on desperately before they give up. Sometimes these battles are the fiercest and bloodiest of the entire war! Some defeated foes keep on fighting because they're out of touch with reality. They ignore all the evidence and delude themselves into thinking they still have a chance. Other defeated foes know they can't win but fight on anyway. They seem to be driven by a vengeful intent to inflict as much pain as they can on the victor before they're forced to surrender.

I'm not sure in which camp of defeated foes Satan belongs. But I am sure that he hasn't laid down his weapons. And for that reason, Peter tells us to arm ourselves with the same purpose that caused Christ to suffer. Christ suffered in order to bring us to God. His atonement satisfied God's righteous wrath against sin so that we could enter His presence. It broke sin's authority to control our behavior. And it guaranteed that one day we'll be free from sin's presence. In bringing us to God, Christ separates us from sin.

Our separation from sin, although assured, is not yet complete. Sin's penalty has been paid and its authority has been broken, but its presence hangs on. The war has been won, but battles still rage. Therefore, we must arm ourselves with Christ's purpose (the reality of our separation from sin) and fight sin's allure. Peter says that we sinned enough before we were saved; now we must have no part of "sensuality, lusts, drunkenness, carousals, drinking parties and abominable idolatries" (4:3).

We can expect the ongoing battles to be fierce and

bloody. Our opponent is strong and not ready to quit. We have the weapons we need to overcome his attacks, but we have to use them if we want to defeat him. If we sit back, relax, and try to coast into heaven, we won't glorify God by following, honoring, and obeying our Lord Jesus Christ.

The great Bible teacher Robert Leighton described our battle like this:

> Although sin is mortally wounded, it still struggles for life and seeks to wound its enemy. It will assault the graces that are in you. . . . So long as you live in the body, traces of your natural corruption remain. So you must be armed against it. Sin will not give you any rest as long as there is one spark of life left in it. This will continue as long as you have life. This old man is stout and will fight to the death. . . . The chains of sin are so strong and so bind our nature that there is no power in us to break free from them until a stronger spirit than our own comes into us. . . . Faith in Christ and the love for him that it brings break through and surmount all difficulties. It is the powerful love of Christ that kills the love of sin and kindles the love of holiness in the soul.[5]

Redemption arms us for battle because it regenerates us. It not only changes our destiny. It changes our hearts. Christ's work on our behalf not only secures our inheritance; it fills us with God's Spirit right here and now. He draws us to Scripture and helps us understand revealed truth about God. The more we learn about Him, the more we will love Him. The more we love Him, the more we will obey Him (John 14:15; 1 John 2:3–6). And the more we obey Him, the more we will separate ourselves from sin.

Separating ourselves from sin in this world increases the impact of our humble witness. Some will be drawn to salvation, but some will be "surprised that [we] do not run with them into the same excess of dissipation, and . . . [will] malign us" (1 Peter 4:4). However, we must not let their hostile reaction dissuade us from fighting. They may win a few skirmishes, but they can't win the war. Peter assures us that "they will give account to Him who is ready to judge the living and the dead. For the gospel has for this purpose been preached even to those who are dead, that though they are judged in the flesh as men, they may live in the spirit according to the will of God" (vv. 5–6).

Those who hear the gospel, see it lived out in the behavior of Christians, and choose to reject it while they are alive will find themselves being judged by it after they die. Their response "in the flesh" to Christ's work of redemption will reveal that our humble witness was for them an aroma of death to death (2 Corinthians 2:14–16).

If you're reading these pages and can't say for sure that you are a Christian, please don't ignore Peter's words about rejecting the gospel. You will give an account to God when you die, and your response to the gospel while you are alive will determine where you spend eternity. If you have not yet accepted Jesus Christ's call to salvation, please read appendix A without delay and ask God in prayer to grant you repentance and the faith to believe.

Notes

1. Joan is not her real name.

2. Edmund Clowney, *The Bible Speaks Today: The Message of 1 Peter*, ed. John R. W. Stott (Downers Grove, Ill.: InterVarsity Press, 1988), 145.

3. Keep in mind that Jesus' promise in Matthew 10:19 was intended to eliminate worry, not preparation.

4. In his commentary on 1 Peter, Peter H. Davids aptly sums up what we can be absolutely sure of when we read 1 Peter 3:19: "In his post resurrection state . . . Christ went somewhere and preached something to certain spirits in some prison" (*The New International Commentary on the New Testament: The First Epistle of Peter,* ed. Ned B. Stonehouse, F. F. Bruce, and Gordon D. Fee [Grand Rapids: Eerdmans, 1990], 138). Then he goes on to say that all of these terms call for an explanation and that a number of alternative interpretations have been given. If you have the time and the inclination to study these various interpretations, I recommend the following commentaries. For a helpful, brief overview of them, see pages 215–17 of Scot McKnight, *The NIV Application Commentary: 1 Peter* (Grand Rapids: Zondervan, 1996). For longer, in-depth discussions, see pages 117–32 of I. Howard Marshall, *The IVP New Testament Commentary Series: 1 Peter,* ed. Grant R. Osborne (Downers Grove, Ill.: InterVarsity Press, 1991); pages 154–68 of Edmund Clowney, *The Bible Speaks Today: The Message of 1 Peter,* ed. John R. W. Stott (Downers Grove, Ill.: InterVarsity Press, 1988); and pages 203–39 of Wayne Grudem, *The Tyndale New Testament Commentaries: 1 Peter* (Grand Rapids: Eerdmans, 1988).

5. Robert Leighton and Griffith Thomas, *The Crossway Classic Commentaries: 1 and 2 Peter,* ed. Alister McGrath and J. I. Packer (Wheaton, Ill.: Crossway, 1999), 179–81.

Exercises

Review

1. What is the essence of Christian humility? What kind of behavior is typically seen in humble Christians? How is humility related to powerful witness?

2. Read Galatians 2:11–21 and describe the way Peter stumbled over a fear of man. How did God use Paul to correct, exhort, and encourage Peter? What connection do you see between Galatians 2:11–21 and 1 Peter 3:13–17?

3. How do we maintain the long-sighted, God-centered perspective that empowers our witness to glorify God? How will those around us respond to our witness when we maintain that perspective?

4. How do we obey Peter's command to always be prepared to give an account for the hope that is in us?

5. Describe the sure basis of Christian confidence.

6. Since Christ's triumph over the power of evil assures us of ultimate victory in our battle with sin, are we free to sit back, relax, and coast into heaven? Explain your answer.

7. How does the fact that redemption regenerates us help in our ongoing battle with sin?

Application

1. Review your memory verses from the previous lesson. Then begin memorizing one or more of the following:

   2 Corinthians 5:21
   Colossians 4:6
   1 Peter 3:15–16

2. This week use Psalm 56:1–13; 2 Corinthians 2:14–16; and Ephesians 5:1–10; 6:10–20 to help you sanctify Christ as Lord in your heart, express your gratitude to

God for His providential care, and develop a readiness to give an account for the hope that is in you.

3. Is your fear of God stronger than your fear of man? To answer this question, think back over the past several weeks and list several occasions when you have interacted with unbelievers. If the unbeliever knew that you are a Christian, did that influence his or her attitude and behavior toward you? Explain. How did your attitude and behavior toward the unbeliever reflect on God? If the unbeliever did not know you are a Christian, did he or she learn of your faith during the encounter? What were your reasons for either revealing or withholding that information? In either case, did this encounter present an opportunity for you to make a defense for the hope that you have? If so, did you take advantage of the opportunity? Explain. Did you do so with gentleness toward the unbeliever and with reverence toward God? If not, explain.

   Summarize what this exercise has revealed to you about whether your fear of God is stronger than your fear of man. List any changes in your attitude or behavior that doing this exercise has shown that you need to make. How, when, where, and in relation to whom will you begin making these changes?

4. Do you believe you are well prepared to make a defense to everyone who asks you to give an account of the hope that you have? If so, on what are you basing your belief? If not, list several activities that will help you become well prepared. Are you willing to commit to pursuing these activities on a regular basis? If so, make a plan detailing precisely what activities you will pursue, when and where you will do them, and who will hold you accountable for doing them. Are you willing to pray

regularly for opportunities to make a defense for the hope that you have? If so, begin immediately.

5. List one or more sins from which you find it difficult to separate yourself. How has this lesson encouraged you to keep fighting the battle against sin?

Digging Deeper

1. How does the fact that our redemption regenerates us relate to our living hope? How can you use a good understanding of this relationship to help yourself and others become better equipped to give an account of the hope that we have?

Primary Passage
1 Peter 4:7–19

Supplementary Passages
Proverbs 10:12; 11:31
Malachi 3:1–6
Matthew 5:11–16; 7:13–14
Luke 12:35–48
John 13:34–35; 14:13–15
Romans 12:4–8
1 Corinthians 12:4–13:10
2 Corinthians 3:18
Ephesians 4:7–16
Philippians 2:1–4
Colossians 1:24; 3:12–17
1 Thessalonians 5:1–11
2 Timothy 3:12
Hebrews 13:1–6
James 5:19–20
1 John 3:13
Revelation 21:1–4

Before reading the lesson material, please read the primary Scripture passage listed above and as many of the supplementary passages as time allows. Then briefly summarize in your notebook what you have read. (Do not go into detail. Limit your summary to a brief description of the people, events, and/or ideas discussed in the passages.)

8

The Cure for
Short-Timer Syndrome

Let us live out of the world as to its spirit, maxim, manners,
but live in it as the sphere of our action and usefulness;
May we be alive to every call of duty,
accepting without question
Thy determination of our circumstances and our service.
—from The Valley of Vision:
A Collection of Puritan Prayers and Devotions

Have you ever suffered from short-timer syndrome? If you've never heard of it, that wouldn't surprise me since I made it up. So, I'll describe the symptoms. Short-timer syndrome afflicts people anticipating a change in their circumstances—particularly those anticipating a change for the better. It causes them to lose interest in now because they're so focused on then. It's a serious malady marked by indifference to daily routines, irresponsible conduct, and an escapist mentality.

I have suffered through and survived at least two bouts of short-timer syndrome. The first occurred during my final month of graduate school. It hit me like a bolt from the blue right after I landed the perfect job. Suddenly, I could not have cared less about the major paper I still had to write or the final exams I still had to take. I had a job. Why sweat the last month of school?

Classes looked pretty dull in light of the real world. Shopping for that new power wardrobe seemed more important than time in the library. And daydreaming about vast new horizons crowded all thoughts of study out of my mind. I knew I was sick, but I wasn't worried. My grades were good enough to guarantee graduation even if I did poorly on my remaining work. In light of my situation, coasting to the finish line seemed entirely appropriate.

My second bout with short-timer syndrome came, ironically, six years later when I decided to resign from that perfect job and become a stay-at-home mom. I gave eight weeks' notice and immediately lost interest in everything on my desk. My mind was so filled with my stay-at-home plans that I was hardly productive during the final two months that my body was parked in the office. To this day, I am grateful that my subsequent work hasn't depended on that ill-used employer's recommendation!

Unfortunately, short-timer syndrome has not been contained in the secular realm. It also invades our spiritual lives. It afflicts Christians by turning their sure inheritance into a distraction. It infects them with the idea that their living hope is a good reason to withdraw from the world instead of the best reason to fulfill their chief end in the world. Christians afflicted with short-timer syndrome spend all their time thinking and talking about what's to come and couldn't care less about giving God glory right here and now. Consequently, their worthy walk tends to disintegrate into an unworthy limp.

God's enemy, Satan, loves it when God's children come down with short-timer syndrome. That's because the affliction takes them out of the battle. Their testimony no longer grates against their godless culture because they're avoiding their culture. They no longer make waves because they're not in the stream. They're huddled together up on the bank. God's enemy, Satan, leaves them alone, because they're right where he wants them—not fighting him.

Peter seems to have sensed that his first-century readers might fall prey to short-timer syndrome. After all, he had splashed a good deal of ink over a long stretch of parchment for the purpose of fortifying their living hope. He had assured them that their inheritance was absolutely secure and that nothing in this world could prevent them from receiving it. He had described the preciousness of their great salvation and affirmed the graciousness of their spiritual resources. He had proclaimed that the war they were fighting had already been won in the triumph of Christ and that they had no reason to doubt ultimate victory. But he wanted them to remember that their living hope was a weapon for fighting ongoing battles—not a license to drift to the sidelines and coast into heaven.

Peter knew that his readers were weary of battle and could therefore be tempted by short-timer syndrome. He knew the incentive of realized future glory could actually distract them from the present pursuit of their chief end. So in the verses we're studying in lesson 8, we'll hear Peter prescribe the unfailing cure for short-timer syndrome: Live now in the light of the end by obeying God joyfully, and exchange shocked surprise at the resultant suffering for expectation of blessing.

Life in Light of the End
(1 Peter 4:7–11)
The first thing we notice about Peter's prescription for short-timer syndrome is that it is grounded in God's gra-

cious gift of living hope to His people. The unfailing cure for short-timer syndrome is not to block out all thought of our sure inheritance as we serve God here on earth. Rather, it is to correctly perceive our inheritance as a motivation for service, not a license for leisure.[1] Peter tells his readers:

> The end of all things is near; therefore, be of sound judgment and sober spirit for the purpose of prayer. Above all, keep fervent in your love for one another, because love covers a multitude of sins. Be hospitable to one another without complaint. As each one has received a special gift, employ it in serving one another as good stewards of the manifold grace of God. Whoever speaks, is to do so as one who is speaking the utterances of God; whoever serves is to do so as one who is serving by the strength which God supplies; so that in all things God may be glorified through Jesus Christ, to whom belongs the glory and dominion forever and ever. Amen.

Do you remember what we learned in lesson 3 about the word *therefore?* If you said it typically marks a transition from doctrine to practice by alerting us to the fact that imperatives are about to follow an encouraging indicative, pat yourself on the back. The word *therefore,* in verse 7, is there for the purpose of telling us to tighten our grip on the preceding indicative before plunging into the upcoming imperatives.

Peter's encouraging indicative is that the end of all things is at hand. "The end of all things" (v. 7) is a reference to our sure inheritance. It alludes to the doctrinal truth that human history is redemptive in purpose and linear in fact. It tells us that a divine hand set all things in motion, guides their progression, and will bring them to a predetermined conclusion—for the purpose of accomplishing divine intention. The divine intention behind human history is displaying God's glory in the redemption of sinners through Jesus Christ.

At the time Peter wrote his first epistle, everything necessary to accomplish the redemption of sinners had come to pass. Jesus Christ had come to earth and lived in perfect conformity to God's holy law. He had paid the penalty for the sins of those God had chosen, and He conquered death in His resurrection. He had ascended to heaven, where He poured forth His Spirit and sat down at the right hand of God to exercise all authority and to intercede for His people.

Most Christians living when Peter wrote were aware of these facts and therefore expected the end to come quickly. That's why they were so vulnerable to short-timer syndrome. Many of them may have been inclined to quit their jobs, sell all their possessions, and sit passively waiting for Jesus' return. Peter writes to exhort them to resist such temptation.

His words are still relevant twenty-one centuries later. Although our hindsight advantage confirms that our first-century brethren weren't short-timers, it doesn't seem to have lessened our vulnerability to short-timer syndrome. I know many Christians who are so caught up in "end-times" speculations that they lose sight of *now* in their concentration on *then*. Peter's unfailing cure for short-timer syndrome instructs us, just as it did them, to view our living hope properly. We must guard against seeing it as an escape hatch justifying irresponsible conduct. Rather, we must see it as a power source fueling God-honoring service.

Bible teacher and historian J. N. D. Kelly says that the indicative truth of the imminent end should be a challenge to watchfulness and irreproachable behavior. He goes on to explain that the last days, in which Christians have been living since the first century, are days of surprise, catastrophe, and testing. Thus they provide opportunity to glorify

God by looking to our living hope for the grace to exhibit quiet confidence, mutual support, and reliance on God.[2]

Peter says Christians who view their living hope properly can't be accused of being so heavenly minded they're no earthly good. In fact, the more heavenly minded they are, the more earthly good they will do. When they correctly view their sure inheritance as a good incentive to obey God's commands, they will fulfill their chief end of joyfully giving God glory as they walk through this world.

They will be wise, sober-minded prayer warriors who cultivate deep communion with God. Their prayers will pour out of hearts saturated with the truth of God's Word. Their prayers will seek strength and guidance from His indwelling Spirit because they understand His sovereign authority and unfailing love. Their prayers will be grounded in the reality of God's divine purposes, not in their daydreams or desperate longings. Their prayers will be driven, nurtured, and colored by their living hope of their sure inheritance.

Christians who pray in that way will love one another. Scot McKnight calls love the "MVP of Christian virtues" and goes on to say that Christians ought to comprise loving communities that look very different from the world around them. Their love for one another should tolerate more differences, forgive more wrongs, and exude more warmth and hospitality.[3] Their love for one another should "stretch out" to seemingly unlimited lengths to encourage and protect one another. It should be patient and kind, not self-seeking, jealous, arrogant, or rude (1 Corinthians 13:4–7).

Their love for one another should make their communities true havens of rest—islands of peaceful refuge from the distress of the world. Peter emphasizes that Christian love is hospitable—not just when it's convenient but whenever it's needed. Christians who love one another readily share food, clothing, and shelter with those who are traveling, impoverished, or simply longing for fellowship. And they do so with no complaints about personal sacrifice.

Christians who pray and love in these ways will also praise God for the spiritual gifts He has given them and rely on His grace to use them effectively. Peter reminds us that all Christians receive spiritual gifts—abilities and talents either specially endowed or spiritually enhanced at salvation.[4] And he exhorts us to humbly exercise them as good stewards of God's multifaceted grace.

Edmund Clowney describes the utter graciousness of spiritual giftedness when he says, "God is to be praised not only for the new birth from which our service begins, but for the continuing grace that enables us, in serving others, to serve Him."[5] Peter summarizes these gifts in the two general categories of speaking and serving and reminds us that good stewardship over them involves exercising them for God's purposes, in His strength, and to His glory.

Thus, we see that Peter's prescription for short-timer syndrome begins with a call to view our living hope properly. But it doesn't stop there. Peter goes on to exhort Christians who suffer for their righteous behavior to exchange shocked surprise for expectation of blessing.

Expect Suffering—and Blessing
(1 Peter 4:12–19)

R. C. Sproul has written an excellent book entitled *Surprised by Suffering*. I can't help but wonder if he got the idea for that title from 1 Peter 4:12. There Peter says, "Beloved, do not be surprised at the fiery ordeal among you, which comes upon you for your testing, as though some strange thing were happening to you."

If you're thinking that title would be a misreading of this verse, let me encourage you to think further. Peter's exhortation doesn't contradict R. C.'s title. Instead, it reflects the uncomfortable fact that most of us nearly always respond to suffering with shocked surprise. If we didn't, Peter would not have had reason to warn us against it. R. C.'s book title insightfully lays bare our need to hear and heed Peter's words.

My experience (and yours too, most likely) bears witness that no matter how sound our theology, no matter how many applicable verses we've memorized, and no matter how eloquently we can state a doctrine of suffering, we are always surprised when it happens to us. We are stunned when the diagnosis of cancer has our name on it. We are shocked when our child is arrested for drug possession. We are astounded when our neighbors and friends label us bigots because of our biblical views on premarital sex, homosexuality, abortion, divorce, and drunkenness. We are struck dumb when audacious terrorists fly commercial airliners into our country's buildings.

Our surprise at suffering increases our vulnerability to short-timer syndrome. First, we recoil, thinking, *This isn't right. This shouldn't have happened to us. We didn't deserve this.* And then we start looking for ways to insulate ourselves from it. We decide that all suffering is inherently bad. We tell ourselves that it couldn't possibly be God's will for us. And we order our lives around protecting ourselves against it.

Why do we do that? Because suffering hurts. And we hate it. Our world is filled to the brim with suffering of one kind or another. And we don't like that at all. We know that there won't be any suffering in heaven. And we like that very much. Quite frankly, we'd rather be there than here. So we take steps to make now seem more like then.

Peter understood our inclination to react to suffering this way, because he had done so himself. When he heard Jesus announce that He "must go to Jerusalem, and suffer many things from the elders and chief priests and scribes, and be killed, and be raised up on the third day," Peter recoiled in horror. And then he attempted to insulate Jesus. He took his Master aside and rebuked Him, saying, "God forbid it, Lord! This shall never happen to You" (Matthew 16:21–22).

Jesus seems to have diagnosed Peter's malady quickly and, in a few stunning words, prescribed the unfailing cure: "Get behind Me, Satan! You are a stumbling block to Me; for you are not setting your mind on God's interests, but man's" (v. 23). Then He went on to explain to all the disciples that true blessing in Christian service does not derive from self-protective attempts to avoid all suffering. Rather, it flows out of self-denial, cross bearing, and following Him. True blessing, according to Jesus, is not saving our earthly lives to gain good in this world but losing our earthly lives, if need be, to gain life everlasting in heaven (vv. 24–26).

Jesus' words seemed to have had a profound impact on Peter. When we read 1 Peter 4:13–19, we hear from a man who's been cured of short-timer syndrome:

> But to the degree that you share the sufferings of Christ, keep on rejoicing; so that also at the revelation of His glory, you may rejoice with exultation. If you are reviled for the name of Christ, you are blessed, because the Spirit of glory and of God rests on you. Make sure that none of you suffers as a murderer, or thief, or evildoer, or a troublesome meddler; but if anyone suffers as a Christian, he is not to be ashamed, but is to glorify God in this name. For it is time for judgment to begin with the household of God; and if it begins with us first, what will be the outcome for those who do not obey the gospel of God? And if it is with difficulty that the righteous is saved, what will become of the godless man and the sinner? Therefore, those also who suffer according to the will of God shall entrust their souls to a faithful Creator in doing what is right.

Peter was no longer setting his mind on man's interests instead of God's. He was proclaiming a God-centered perspective of suffering: one that sees it as ordained by and for divine purpose and as the inevitable fruit of identification with Christ. Peter tells us that sharing in the sufferings of Christ is cause for rejoicing. Why? Because it provides opportunity to strengthen our faith by exercising it in difficult circumstances. And because it testifies of our union with Christ and thus intensifies our living hope of sharing His glory.

Peter's perspective tells us that being abused for identifying ourselves with Christ is a blessing. Kenneth Wuest elaborates on that startling idea by explaining that the Greek word for blessed means "prosperous" and that persecution reflects the extent of our spiritual prosperity.[6] The more prosperous our spirituality, the more it grates on the world and the more sparks it throws off. But in the process, it also emits a pleasing aroma to God (2 Corinthians 2:14). And He responds by causing His Spirit to "rest" (1 Peter 4:14) upon us—equipping us to carry our burdens and walk worthy of our high calling in Christ.

God's indwelling Spirit blesses us with the ability to view our living hope properly. D. A. Carson says that the ability to transcend present pain by reflecting on future glory "means that [Christians] do not always have ready answers; they have, instead, a reasonable confidence in One who does have the answers and the power to impose them. God will have the last word; we dare to wait for that."[7]

Peter's perspective on suffering tells us that those who suffer for doing wrong cannot expect to be blessed, but that those who suffer because they are Christians should glorify God. Why glorify God when we suffer as Christians? Because we recognize that the end of all things is at hand. The accomplishment of full redemption could come at any moment. Our suffering for righteousness sake tells us that God's judgment has begun as refining fire in the midst of

His people. Suffering purifies God's church and helps conform us to the image of Christ.

God's refining fire will eventually spread beyond the bounds of His church to judge those who have rejected His mercy and refused to obey Him. Peter quotes Proverbs 11:31 to emphasize the destructiveness of this spreading fire. If enduring refining fire in God's church seems painfully difficult, how catastrophic will be enduring judgmental fires in the world!

Life in light of the end could get more intense as the final judgment draws near. And we just might be tempted by short-timer syndrome. Peter exhorts us to resist falling prey to its allure by consciously entrusting our souls to a faithful Creator in doing what is right. Robert Leighton aptly summarized Peter's command when he said that the key to true Christian tranquility in times of trouble is to look upward and forward. We are to look upward to the good hand of God because "there is much strength in being persuaded of the power of God." And we are to look forward to the end of our journey where our sure inheritance waits.[8]

Boiled down to its essence, that's the unfailing cure for short-timer syndrome.

Notes

1. I urge you to dig deeper into this important concept by reading Bryan Chapell's fine book, *Holiness by Grace: Delighting in the Joy That Is Our Strength* (Wheaton, Ill.: Crossway, 2001).

2. J. N. D. Kelly, *Black's New Testament Commentaries: The Epistles of Peter and Jude,* ed. Henry Chadwick (London: A&C Black, 1969; Peabody, Mass.: Hendrickson, 1969), 177.

3. Scot McKnight, *The NIV Application Commentary: 1 Peter* (Grand Rapids: Zondervan, 1996), 245.

4. Michael Bentley, *Living for Christ in a Pagan World: 1 and 2 Peter Simply Explained,* The Welwyn Commentary Series (Durham, England: Evangelical Press, 1990), 150.

5. Edmund Clowney, *The Bible Speaks Today: The Message of 1 Peter,* ed. John R. W. Stott (Downers Grove, Ill.: InterVarsity Press, 1988), 187.

6. Kenneth S. Wuest, *Wuest's Word Studies from the Greek New Testament,* vol. 2, *Philippians, Hebrews, The Pastoral Epistles, First Peter, In These Last Days* (Grand Rapids: Eerdmans, 1973), 120.

7. D. A. Carson, *How Long, O Lord? Reflections on Suffering and Evil* (Grand Rapids: Baker, 1990), 151.

8. Robert Leighton and Griffith Thomas, *The Crossway Classic Commentaries: 1 and 2 Peter,* ed. Alister McGrath and J. I. Packer (Wheaton, Ill.: Crossway, 1999), 220–21.

Exercises

Review

1. Describe short-timer syndrome in your own words. Then explain how short-timer syndrome invades our spiritual lives. *Losing interest in the present in anticipation of future*

2. State the two elements of Peter's prescription for short-timer syndrome. *See it as motivation for service, not license for leisure.*

3. What is the word *therefore* in 1 Peter 4:7 there for? *Transition from doctrine to practice*

4. Explain the importance of viewing our living hope properly. Describe the behavior (thoughts, attitudes, and actions) that characterizes Christians who view their living hope properly. *View it as a power source fueling God-honoring service*

5. How does being surprised by suffering increase our vulnerability to short-timer syndrome? *We concentrate on future - forget now.*

6. Describe, in your own words, the God-centered perspective of suffering that Peter proclaims in 1 Peter 4:13–19. Include in your description an explanation of the joy and blessing to be found in suffering righteously.

7. According to Robert Leighton, what is the key to Christian tranquility in times of trouble? Do you agree with him? Explain your answer.

   Look upward + forward

Application

1. Review your memory verses from the previous lesson. Then begin memorizing one or more of the following:

   John 13:34–35
   2 Corinthians 3:18
   Philippians 2:1–4

2. This week use Psalms 13; 46; 73; Matthew 5:11–16; and Ephesians 4:7–16 to help you pray for the ability to view your living hope properly and to use it as an effective tool to glorify God in the midst of difficulty and suffering.

3. Have you ever suffered from short-timer syndrome? If so, describe your particular bout with this affliction. Is this an unusual affliction for you or something you seem to deal with on a regular basis? If you seem particularly

vulnerable to short-timer syndrome, how will Peter's prescription help you combat it? List specific examples of changes you will make in your behavior (thoughts, attitudes, and actions) in regard to living now in light of the end and exchanging shock for expectation of blessing when you face suffering.

4. The Greek word *peirasmos* is usually translated by the English words *trial* or *test*. It often describes a difficult circumstance that can be either a temptation aimed at the destruction of faith or an opportunity to strengthen faith by exercising it in adversity. Whether the circumstance becomes a temptation or an opportunity depends, almost entirely, on the way we respond to it.

   Describe a difficult circumstance you have encountered recently and the way you responded to it. At the time you encountered this *peirasmos,* did it seem more like a temptation aimed at destroying your faith or an opportunity to strengthen your faith? Do you believe that your actual response to the circumstance weakened or strengthened your faith? How might the truths you learned in this lesson help you respond to future difficulties as opportunities instead of temptations?

Digging Deeper

1. In *God in the Wasteland,* David Wells said, "The choice for God now has to become one in which the church begins to form itself, by his grace and truth, into an outcropping of counter-cultural spirituality. It must first recover the sense of antithesis between Christ and culture and then find ways to sustain that antithesis. . . . It must give up self-cultivation for self-surrender, entertainment for worship, intuition for truth, slick marketing for authentic witness, success for faithfulness, power

for humility, a God bought on cheap terms for the God who calls us to costly obedience. It must, in short, be willing to do God's business on God's terms" (*God in the Wasteland: The Reality of Truth in a World of Fading Dreams* [Grand Rapids: Eerdmans, 1994], 223).

Discuss Dr. Wells's exhortation to the church in light of Peter's instruction in 1 Peter 4:7–19.

2. Study 1 Peter 4:7–11 and then write a concise explanation of what Peter means when he says "love covers a multitude of sins."

Primary Passage
1 Peter 5

Supplementary Passages
Deuteronomy 31:6
Job 1:1–12
Psalm 37:1–11; 55:22
Proverbs 4:13–27
Ezekiel 34:1–10
Micah 6:8
Zechariah 3:1–5
Matthew 6:25–34
Mark 10:42–45
John 13:1–9; 21:15–17
2 Corinthians 11:14
Ephesians 6:10–20
Philippians 4:6
James 4:6–9

Before reading the lesson material, please read the primary Scripture passage listed above and as many of the supplementary passages as time allows. Then briefly summarize in your notebook what you have read. (Do not go into detail. Limit your summary to a brief description of the people, events, and/or ideas discussed in the passages.)

LESSON **9**

The Team Concept of Humble Servants

The prince of darkness grim,
We tremble not for him;
His rage we can endure,
For lo! his doom is sure,
One little word shall fell him.
—Martin Luther

On February 3, 2002, the New England Patriots defeated the St. Louis Rams in Super Bowl XXXVI. It was quite a shock. Although New England had lots of fans on that day, few of them actually thought they would be cheering a winner. By halftime, however, they were beginning to hope. New England was ahead 14–3, and their fans were thinking, *Maybe, just maybe.* But then the Rams came roaring back late in the second half to tie the score at 17–17. Everyone thought that, for the first time in Super Bowl history, the game was headed for overtime. Everyone, that is, except the Patriots. Refusing to run out the clock, they moved down field in the final seconds and kicked a stunning forty-eight-yard field goal as time expired.

The media coverage hailed the game as one of football's biggest upsets, and the experts theorized about how the Patriots did it. Although I am no expert, I have my own theory. And as you've probably guessed, it leads right into a discussion of 1 Peter 5:1–14.

My nonexpert theory is that the Patriots' win had a lot to do with their team image. Obviously, both teams had ability. And both teams had played hard and well during the season. The experts, however, gave the Rams a big edge and touted the Patriots as not-a-chance underdogs. Every football aficionado on the face of the planet seemed to believe them—except the not-a-chance underdogs.

The New England Patriots played like a team who'd never heard the word *underdog.* My guess is they hadn't been listening to the experts but to their coach, Bill Belichick. I have no idea what Belichick had been telling them, but I'm fairly certain he hadn't labeled them losers. Whatever he said built a winning-team image. They hit the field with a team spirit of unity and engaged their opponents with a team vision of victory. Each Patriot player saw himself as an integral part of a winning team. *Maybe, just maybe,* that's how they did it.

So what does all this have to do with 1 Peter 5:1–14? Simply this. Each believer in Christ is also an integral part of a winning team. And it's essential that we build and maintain a winning-team image. Life on this earth involves daily combat with the world, the flesh, and the devil—opponents more deadly than rival athletes. And that daily combat is surely no game. The stakes are much higher than the Vince Lombardi trophy. If we listen to and believe what the world says about us, we won't stand a chance of fulfilling our chief end.

We need to tune out the world and heed our Lord Jesus Christ, who speaks to us through His servant Peter. In the closing words of his first letter, Peter helps us build a winning-team image. He exhorts us to take on the world with a team spirit of unity—the fruit of humility. And he commands us to live in this world with a team vision of victory—the fruit of living hope.

The Team Spirit of Unity: The Fruit of Humility
(1 Peter 5:1–7)

The New England Patriots displayed their team spirit of unity in Super Bowl XXXVI by being introduced as a team instead of spotlighting their team leaders and stars. That attention-getting break with tradition spoke volumes about their team image. It emphasized the whole team's commitment to a common cause. It also reflected the humility of their team leaders and stars.

Humility is a difficult virtue to cultivate, particularly for those who are team leaders and stars. That's because team leaders and stars stand out from the crowd. They are talented, gifted, skilled, and effective. They are self-starters who confidently step up and take charge of people and circumstances. They boldly go into uncharted territory and motivate others to come along with them. They are admired, looked up to, and respected by others. Team leaders and stars are exceptional people. And consequently, they're more inclined to be proud than to be humble.

Proud team leaders and stars can destroy a team spirit of unity. They do that when they stand in the spotlight that should be focused on the team's common cause. But that doesn't mean that teams shouldn't have leaders and stars. Without their exceptional talents and gifts, a team's common cause tends to disintegrate into vague dreams and lame effort. Effective teams need leaders and stars. But they don't need proud ones. They need leaders and stars who have learned to be humble.

Peter was a team leader and star who had learned to be humble. He had learned it from Jesus, who was also a team leader and star who had learned to be humble (Luke 2:51–52; Philippians 2:8; Hebrews 5:8). Jesus taught His disciples humility through His words and His example. He admonished them not to follow the example of those Gentile rulers who lord it over those under their authority, but to pattern their leadership style after His. "The Son of Man did not come to be served, but to serve, and to give His life a ransom for many," Jesus told His disciples (Mark 10:45). And then He showed them how to be servant leaders by washing their feet (John 13:1–5). Servant leaders are those who spotlight the church's common cause of giving God glory. They do that by submitting themselves to God's will, no matter how humbling that submission might be.

Peter had proudly resisted that lesson in servant leadership, but Jesus had humbly insisted he learn it. "If I do not wash you, you have no part with Me," Jesus told him (John 13:8). Jesus was emphasizing that Peter's redemption depended upon his Savior's humble submission to God and that Peter's call to lead leaders demanded that he go and do likewise. Peter obviously got the message. Right then and there he offered Jesus his hands and head for washing as well as his feet (v. 9). And years later he taught church leaders scattered throughout Pontus, Galatia, Cappadocia, Asia, and Bithynia the same leadership principles that Jesus taught him.

> Therefore, I exhort the elders among you, as your fellow elder and witness of the sufferings of Christ, and a partaker also of the glory that is to be revealed, shepherd the flock of God among you, exercising oversight not under compulsion, but voluntarily, according to the will of God; not for sordid gain, but with eagerness; nor yet as lording it over those allotted to your charge, but proving to be examples to the flock. And when the Chief Shepherd appears, you will receive the unfading crown of glory. (1 Peter 5:1–4)

Jesus had taught Peter to "feed the flock" by word and example just as He had done. Jesus (unlike some parents) told His disciples in essence, "Do as I say *and* do as I do." Then He told them to pass on His instruction to others (John 13:12–15). And Peter obeyed Him. When he addressed church leaders, Peter not only told them to shepherd by example; he patterned the behavior he wanted them to produce. Peter didn't lord his apostolic authority over them. Rather, he exhorted them as a fellow elder, sufferer, and partaker of glory. This once proud team leader and star who had learned to be humble didn't stand in the spotlight. He stood shoulder to shoulder with other leaders and helped them turn the spotlight on their common cause.

Shepherding the flock of God isn't about self-exaltation. It's about helping others glorify God. Church leaders do that by imitating the Chief Shepherd, their Lord Jesus Christ. They humble themselves under God's will and see themselves not as rulers but as servants of those allotted to their charge. Peter says they should serve the flock voluntarily, with selfless eagerness, and in an exemplary manner. They should not give the impression that they're serving "under compulsion" (5:2) and if given a choice would quickly do something else. They should not appear to be serving for "sordid gain" (v. 2), putting their personal benefit ahead of those they are leading. And they should never abuse their God-given authority by coercing, threatening, or intimidating the sheep.

Humble church leaders don't stand in the spotlight. Instead they stand behind it and make sure it stays focused on the team's common cause of giving God glory. Church leaders who do that willingly, eagerly, and gently exchange the fading glory of acclaim in this world for the unfading crown of glory in the world to come. They model, for their flock, the great wisdom of humble submission to God. And our teacher Peter says that the flock should in turn imitate their example.

You younger men, likewise, be subject to your elders; and all of you, clothe yourselves with humility toward one another, for God is opposed to the proud, but gives grace to the humble. Therefore humble yourselves under the mighty hand of God, that He may exalt you at the proper time, casting all your anxiety on Him, because He cares for you. (1 Peter 5:5–7)

There is some disagreement among commentators about what Peter meant by the term "younger men."[1] Many (with whom I agree) believe he was admonishing the congregation as a whole to humbly submit to godly leaders who humbly submit to God. Everyone in the congregation is to be clothed in humility. The leaders model submission to God as they serve the flock, and the flock imitates them by serving each other. The pattern Peter lays out cultivates a team spirit of unity. It calls everyone to join hands in submitting to God, looking to Him for exaltation, trusting Him in trouble, and rejoicing in His perfect care. No one is to stand in the spotlight and blur the team's focus on its common cause.

J. N. D. Kelly says that the essence of self-humbling is entrusting oneself and one's troubles to God.[2] Kelly emphasizes that mutual self-humbling in a congregation spawns a sense of solidarity in Christ that motivates strong resistance to opposition.[3] That happens because "Christians can trust the *power* of the Lord, for his hand is mighty; they can trust the *faithfulness* of the Lord, for their cares are his concerns."[4]

Humbling ourselves under God's mighty hand fills us with bold confidence as it dissolves fear and worry. When we marinate our minds in His wisdom, accept our circumstances as ordained by His providence, and see ourselves as His perfectly loved children, we will, quite naturally, cast all our anxiety upon Him.

All our anxiety is rooted in pride. If that's a new thought for you, think with me for a while. Anxiety screams that we've taken over the reins of our lives and stopped trusting God. It shouts that our circumstances have bolted out of control and God hasn't curbed them to our satisfaction. And it orders Him to shove over and give us a shot at it. Anxiety puts us in the spotlight and blinds us to the fact of God's sovereign care.

Peter reminds us that God opposes the proud who grab the reins in anxiety and that He gives grace to the humble who trust in His care. The present tense verbs Peter uses assure us that opposing the proud and giving grace to the humble are continuous actions. Therefore, humbling ourselves under God's mighty hand goes beyond our initial salvation to become our way of life. Robert Leighton, with poetic eloquence, describes the Christian's lifestyle of humble submission like this: "God's sweet dews and showers of grace slide off the mountains of pride, fall on the low valleys of humble hearts, and make them pleasant and fertile."[5]

Humble submission to God opens the door to His grace, which equips us to live to the glory of God. When a congregation follows Peter's instruction and serves each other in humble submission to God, they build a team spirit of unity that promotes a team vision of victory.

The Team Vision of Victory:
The Fruit of Living Hope
(1 Peter 5:8–14)

Though the New England Patriots were confident they could defeat the powerful St. Louis Rams, they didn't relax or doze off during the game. They knew they were fighting an adversary who wouldn't give up until the last second. And if they wanted to win, they would have to combine their assurance of victory with diligent effort.

That is exactly the way Peter said Christians should engage the devil. Although we know we can beat him (because we are in Christ), we dare not underestimate him. He is a powerful adversary who hates God with a passion. He knows he's already been beaten in the triumph of Christ, and that knowledge adds fuel to his fiery rage. He despises the fact that despite his best efforts, God accomplished salvation to the praise of His glory. And he lashes out against the painful reality that he can't take from God's children what they have been given.

God's grace surrounds us as an impregnable fortress. It is our living hope of our sure inheritance. Because salvation is gracious, we do nothing to earn it and we do nothing to keep it. Salvation depends wholly, completely, from start to finish, upon God's unchangeable, undefeatable power and love. God accomplished salvation that way because it displays His glory most fully. And Satan kicks hard against the goad of the knowledge that he can't stop, steal, or repeal the finished work of salvation.

He roars in outrage and with breathtaking fury attacks a new front. Since salvation's grace fortress is absolutely secure, he prowls about seeking ways to dim, mar, and disrupt the display of God's glory here on this earth. Peter tells us to respect his ferocity, not because he can cost us the ultimate victory but because he can weaken our common cause.

Keep in mind that our common cause here on this earth is *not* laying claim to our sure inheritance. Jesus Christ has already laid claim to it for us. Our common cause on this earth is giving God glory. Nothing can prevent us from receiving our sure inheritance. But diabolic assaults from the world, the flesh, and the devil can deface the beauty of our spiritual house and hamper the proclamation of our Father's excellencies. Our living hope is secure regardless of our behavior. But our common cause is imperiled when we fail to be diligent.

Peter warns us against relaxing in our living hope and dozing off while the enemy is prowling about. He reminds us that the fruit of our living hope isn't spiritual laziness. Rather, it is a team vision of victory encompassing healthy respect for our adversary's abilities as well as bold confidence in the true grace of God.

> Be of sober spirit, be on the alert. Your adversary, the devil, prowls around like a roaring lion, seeking someone to devour. But resist him, firm in your faith, knowing that the same experiences of suffering are being accomplished by your brethren who are in the world. And after you have suffered for a little while, the God of all grace, who called you to His eternal glory in Christ, will Himself perfect, confirm, strengthen and establish you. To Him be dominion forever and ever. Amen. (5:8–11)

Throughout his first letter, Peter has emphasized the equipping nature of grace. And his closing words to scattered Christians facing all manner of persecution hammer that point home again. He wants his readers to understand so as to appropriate the indicative truth that grace does more than save us at the beginning of our Christian lives and glorify us at the end. It also enables us to walk worthy of our high calling during the time in between.

God doesn't save us, assure us of future glory in heaven, and then say, "Life is going to be pretty rough. But I've done my part. Run the race as best you can, and I'll see you at the finish line." But a lot of us live like that's what He's done. We gladly proclaim that justification and glorification are all of grace, but we live as if sanctification is all of our effort. Living like that doesn't fulfill our high calling because it turns the spotlight away from God's glory and shines it on us.

Peter asserts that our common cause is best served by remaining alert and resisting satanic attack, firm in our faith. Bible commentators debate whether Peter was talking about objective faith (the body of Christian doctrine) or subjective faith (personal belief). But since Peter was such a practical theologian, I have a hunch he was referring to both.

Our personal belief in God's gracious promise to sustain us in trouble is rooted in His gracious revelation of doctrinal truth. Subjective faith grounded in objective faith equips us to resist the prowling lion who seeks to devour us. Robert Leighton comments that faith sets the stronger Lion of Judah against the roaring lion of the bottomless pit, and then assures us that "the delivering Lion opposes and defeats the devouring lion."[6]

Objective faith teaches that although the devouring lion is free to prowl, his range of motion is securely tethered to the outworking of God's ultimate purposes (Job 1:6–12). And it also tells us that he is not free to tempt us beyond our ability to bear (1 Corinthians 10:13). Subjective faith understands so as to appropriate that God's mighty hand sets boundaries on the extent and duration of Satan's activities and equips us to resist his temptations so that God gets the glory.

Both objective and subjective faith are gifts of God's grace (Ephesians 2:8–10; 2 Peter 1:1) that we are commanded to take up and use in pursuit of our common cause (Ephesians 6:10–20). Peter's perspective on Christian living is clear: We have everything we need in our faith to glorify God here on this earth. But we have to use what we have been given. Our living hope of our sure inheritance cultivates a team vision of victory that sparks energetic resistance to our powerful adversary. If we want to walk worthy of our high calling in Christ, we dare not relax and doze off in the midst of battle.

Edmund Clowney affirms that because Peter's witness is true, his encouragement is real.[7] Objective faith, quickened in our hearts and minds by the Holy Spirit, gives birth to subjective faith that equips us to stand firmly on the solid ground of God's promises. We modern-day readers of Peter's letter need to heed his advice just as much as did his first-century readers. Clowney says we must not cling "to an impersonal moral code, nor to philosophical abstractions . . . [but] to the grace of God; not what [we] have done for God, but what God has done for [us] in Christ."[8]

"This is the true grace of God," Peter proclaims. "Stand firm in it!" (5:12).

Notes

1. Some commentators believe Peter was distinguishing between two leadership groups composed of older and younger men. Some believe he wasn't referring to leadership groups but to older and younger elements of the congregation. And some (with whom I agree) believe he was addressing ruling elders and those they rule.

2. J. N. D. Kelly, *Black's New Testament Commentaries: The Epistles of Peter and Jude,* ed. Henry Chadwick (London: A&C Black, 1969; Peabody, Mass.: Hendrickson, 1969), 208.

3. Ibid., 211.

4. Ibid.

5. Robert Leighton and Griffith Thomas, *The Crossway Classic Commentaries: 1 and 2 Peter,* ed. Alister McGrath and J. I. Packer (Wheaton, Ill.: Crossway, 1999), 231.

6. Ibid., 243.

7. Edmund Clowney, *The Bible Speaks Today: The Message of 1 Peter,* ed. John R. W. Stott (Downers Grove, Ill.: InterVarsity Press, 1988), 223.

8. Ibid.

Exercises

Review

1. Discuss the importance of Christians developing and maintaining a winning-team image. Of what should this image consist, and what should be its focus? Read 1 Corinthians 15:9–10; 2 Corinthians 3:1–6; 9:8; and Philippians 2:12–13. How would a winning-team image based on our confidence in ourselves differ from a winning-team image based on our confidence in Christ?

2. Describe the connection between Christian unity and humility. What evidence do we have in 1 Peter 5:1–14 that Peter had learned the lessons in humility that Jesus had taught him? If you see evidence in other parts of 1 Peter, list that as well.

3. How should church leaders display humility in their leadership roles? Discuss the importance of church leaders exercising their God-given authority with genuine humility. What problems and difficulties arise when church leaders exercise authority devoid of humility? How does the church as a whole benefit when church leaders exercise authority in a humble manner?

4. In your own words, describe or illustrate J. N. D. Kelly's

definition of the essence of self-humbling (page 150). Then explain the statement, "All our anxiety is rooted in pride." Relate this statement to Peter's command to "humble yourselves under the mighty hand of God . . . casting all your anxiety on Him, because He cares for you" (5:6–7). Include an explanation of how humbling ourselves under God's mighty hand fills us with confidence.

5. Based upon what you have learned in 1 Peter, explain what you believe God's purposes are in opposing the proud and giving grace to the humble.

6. Discuss the danger of Christians underestimating their adversary, the devil.

7. What is our common cause here on this earth? What does Peter's perspective on Christian living say about accomplishing our common cause here on this earth?

8. Distinguish between objective and subjective faith. Support the idea that Peter may be referring to both kinds of faith in 1 Peter 5:9.

9. Drawing on what you have learned in 1 Peter, write a short explanation of what Peter means when he says, "This is the true grace of God. Stand firm in it!" (5:12).

Application

1. Review your memory verses from the previous lesson. Then begin memorizing one or more of the following:

   Micah 6:8
   1 Corinthians 10:12–13
   1 Peter 5:6–7

2. This week in your prayer time, use Psalm 37; 1 Peter 5:6–7; and Ephesians 6:10–20 to help you humble yourself under God's mighty hand, cast all your anxiety on Him, and resist the devil as you go about your daily activities.

3. The great seventeenth-century Bible teacher and pastor Robert Leighton described the "true temperament of a true child of God" to be one of humble confidence. This unique (to Christians) ability to combine lowliness and boldness results from the privilege of casting all our worries, fears, and cares upon God because we know (for a fact, without doubt) that He loves us and will always take the best possible care of us. Developing and maintaining this "true temperament" is important because it glorifies God by reflecting His true character to those around us.

   Spend some time this week examining yourself to see if you consistently reflect this "true temperament of a true child of God." Do this by honestly answering the following questions after reading and meditating on the indicative truths contained in the verses that follow them.

   Do I truly believe that God sovereignly controls all circumstances of life? (Psalms 115:1–3; 135:5–6; Ecclesiastes 7:13–14; Isaiah 14:24, 27; 40:12–18, 21–31; 43:13; 45:5–7, 9; 46:8–11; Romans 9:19–24; 11:33–36)

   Do I truly believe that God loves me more than anyone else does—even more than I love myself—and that He does indeed work in all circumstances of life to glorify Himself and benefit me? (Deuteronomy 10:12–13; Psalms 37; 73; 103; Isaiah 43:1–7; Lamentations 3:21–32; Romans 8:28–39; 2 Corinthians 1:3–4; 9:8; Philippians 4:13, 19; Hebrews 13:5–6; 1 John 4:7–17)

   Do I truly believe that worry is sinful because it misrepresents God's power and love to those around me and consequently fails to glorify Him? (Psalm 46:1–3, 10–11; Isaiah 41:9–10, 13; Matthew 6:19–34; Philippians 4:4–9; 1 Peter 5:6–7)

Does my behavior (thoughts, attitudes, and actions) typically reflect biblical truth about God's love and care of His children? (Joshua 1:1–9; Matthew 5:13–16; 7:24–27; Romans 6:12–14; Ephesians 4:1–3, 11–16; Colossians 1:9–12; 3:16–17; James 1:22–25; 1 John 4:4, 18–19)

If you cannot honestly answer yes to each of the above questions, ask God in prayer to help you determine whether you are failing to truly believe His revealed truth about His power and love or to behave consistently with what you believe. Once you have made this determination, seek the advice and counsel of a church leader or mature Christian friend, mentor, or relative who is willing to help you develop a "true temperament" of humble confidence in your walk with the Lord.

4. List several activities that, if practiced habitually, will enhance your ability to resist the devil, firm in your faith. Which of these activities do you currently practice habitually? Make a specific, step-by-step plan that will help you begin practicing one or more of those you are not currently practicing habitually. Implement your plan this week.

Digging Deeper

1. In a sermon entitled "The Weight of Glory," C. S. Lewis said, "The New Testament has lots to say about self-denial, but not about self-denial as an end in itself. . . . Indeed, if we consider the unblushing promises of reward and the staggering nature of the rewards promised in the Gospels, it would seem that Our Lord finds our

desires not too strong, but too weak. We are half-hearted creatures, fooling around with drink and sex and ambition when infinite joy is offered us, like an ignorant child who wants to go on making mud pies in a slum because he cannot imagine what is meant by the offer of a holiday at the sea. We are far too easily pleased" (*The Weight of Glory and Other Addresses* [Grand Rapids: Eerdmans, 1965], 1–2).

Relate Lewis's words to the following purpose statement for 1 Peter: Stand firm in the true grace of God!

PART 2

Grace to Grow

Those who are not rooted in knowledge by clear information and frequent meditation of the truth and have not their hearts established with grace by the frequent exercise thereof, will readily be a prey to soul-deceivers.
—Alexander Nisbet

Primary Passage
2 Peter 1:1–11

Supplementary Passages
Isaiah 43:1–15
John 1:1–14; 8:31–32; 17; 20:24–31
Romans 8
1 Corinthians 2:4–5; 6:19–20
2 Corinthians 4:1–18
Galatians 2:20
Philippians 2:12–13; 3:7–14
Colossians 1:25–29; 2:9–10
1 Timothy 1:5, 12–14
James 2:14–26
1 John 4:20–21; 5:11–13

Before reading the lesson material, please read the primary Scripture passage listed above and as many of the supplementary passages as time allows. Then briefly summarize in your notebook what you have read. (Do not go into detail. Limit your summary to a brief description of the people, events, and/or ideas discussed in the passages.)

10

The Key Weapon in the War on God's Word

Unless God's Word illumines the way, the whole life of man is wrapped in darkness and mist, so that they cannot but miserably stray. —John Calvin

As providence would have it, I attended Ligonier Ministries' 2002 national conference in Orlando, Florida, the week before I started writing part 2 of this study. Interestingly, the theme for the conference was *War on the Word,* a phrase that summarizes Peter's second epistle. I do not believe that was a coincidence.

The sermons I heard at the conference touched on nearly everything Peter teaches in his second epistle. They affirmed the authority and centrality of God's Word in our lives and warned of the dangers of insidious heresy. They called for renewed commitment to application-minded Bible study and for strengthened defenses against smooth-talking false teachers. They proclaimed that a Christian worldview, forged in the true knowledge of God, is our surest weapon in the war on the Word and is therefore essential to living out our salvation.

In essence, the men I heard preach in Orlando spotlighted Peter's indicative that God's Word is truth, recorded by "men moved by the Holy Spirit [who] spoke from God" (2 Peter 1:21). And they emphasized the importance of obeying Peter's imperative to "grow in grace and knowledge of our Lord and Savior Jesus Christ" (3:18). I thank God for providentially ordering my circumstances so that I would have the benefit of hearing them preach before I started to write.

Peter wrote both of his epistles to Christians at war.[1] He wrote as a practical theologian whose primary purpose was not to define a doctrine of suffering but to put in the hands of beleaguered believers much-needed weapons. He armed them with the living hope of their sure inheritance and encouraged them to stand firm in God's glorious grace. He assured them that the war had already been won in the triumph of Christ, although their enemy, Satan, had not yet surrendered. He reminded them that defeated foes often fight fiercely on and that they should not be surprised by their ongoing assaults. And he urged them to prepare for combat on two critical fronts: intense persecution from the world around them and cunning false teaching from inside their assemblies.

We have already studied Peter's first letter, in which he exhorts us to "stand firm" in the true grace of God as we face persecution. And now we turn our attention to his second letter, in which he calls us to active duty in the war on the Word. Peter's marching orders are clear in this brief epistle: Steadfastly proclaim, live out, and defend the truth of God's Word. And his accompanying battle cry is as daunting as it is demanding: Be bold in combating false teaching by growing in grace and in the knowledge of our Lord Jesus Christ.

Although it is obvious that engaging the enemy in the war on the Word will be no easy task, Peter seems to assume that no true believer will duck the draft. We know active duty will surely cost us comfort, leisure, and ease. We know it may alienate a few friends, divide our families, or label us rigid, intolerant, and even unloving. We know it might make us the targets of abuse or attack. We know, after all, that it is a war. But we also know it's a war that is necessary and well worth any sacrifice.

The war on the Word is assault on God's truth. And God's truth is foundational to living out our salvation. We cannot stand firm and grow in the true grace of God on a crumbling foundation (Psalm 11:3). We cannot walk worthy of our high calling without contending earnestly for the faith once for all delivered to us in Scripture (Jude 3). We cannot enjoy peace with God if we compromise truth for the sake of peace in this world (Jeremiah 6:13–15; John 17:15–17). And we cannot glorify God without magnifying His Word in accord with His name (Psalm 138:2).

Peter says that the war on the Word will be fought and won by honing and wielding the sword of the Spirit, which is the true knowledge of God revealed in the Bible (Ephesians 6:17). In the opening verses of his second epistle, he describes the essential qualities of this indispensable weapon. In verses 1–4, he affirms that true knowledge of God converts and equips us for battle. Then, in verses 5–11, he explains how it spurs us to fight valiantly and assures us of victory.

True Knowledge Converts and Equips
(2 Peter 1:1–4)

Peter opens his second epistle with a clear declaration that the essential weapon in the war on the Word is true knowledge of God. And he does so in a way that reveals that his grace-conscious, grace-filled, and grace-dependent perspective of Christian living had not changed a bit since he wrote his first letter. In verse 1, he affirms that saving faith is not only inseparable from the true knowledge of what

God has done for us through Jesus Christ. It is also a free gift of God's sovereign grace. And in verses 2–4, he describes our equipping for battle in terms of grace and peace being multiplied in the true knowledge of God.

He begins by introducing himself as "Simon Peter, a bond-servant and apostle of Jesus Christ" (v. 1)—a self-portrait depicting his grace-laden view of his salvation. He saw himself as a new creation in Christ—a man who, by God's grace alone, had been truly transformed. Proud, self-centered Simon had been redeemed and regenerated. He had become humble, Christ-centered Peter, a servant leader devoted to proclaiming, living out, and defending the truth of God's Word.

He addresses his letter to "those who have received a faith of the same kind as ours, by the righteousness of our God and Savior, Jesus Christ" (v. 2)—in other words, to those who share with him the indescribable blessing of gracious salvation. His greeting extends beyond the first century to embrace all believers in Jesus Christ. He is talking to me. And he is talking to you. He declares that all believers are undeniably saved through their faith in the truth, but he also affirms that our faith was not our contribution to our salvation. He says that we "received" (v. 1) the faith we needed to believe and trust in God's truth. Our faith wasn't ours until we received it, as a free gift of God.[2]

Most commentators agree that Peter is talking about subjective faith (the belief and trust that responds to the gospel) instead of objective faith (the truth that makes up the gospel). He is making the point that salvation is gracious from start to finish—that it is all of God and none of us. Even the faith to respond to God's truth is given to us by Him. All that we do "to be saved" is exercise the faith we are graciously given (John 6:28–29; Acts 16:31). And even that exercise is motivated by God (John 6:44, 63, 65).

Our lost condition is a little like standing in a refreshing spring rain without any awareness that we are thirsty. The part of our brains that tells us we need water has been damaged so badly, it no longer works. Without medical intervention, we will die of thirst even while pure water is drenching us to the skin. As long as we don't know that we need the water to live, we don't see its value and may even think it a nuisance. But if someone comes to our rescue, intervenes with appropriate medical aid, and awakens us to our need, we see the rain in a new light—and acutely sense our desperation. We now have a taste for the water and want it intensely, but have no cup to collect it. Since we are devoid of resources, we can't make or buy a cup, so we cry out for help to the same person who enabled us to see our need. If we can be given a cup, we can access the rain.

The Someone who comes to our aid is, of course, God. The refreshing spring rain is His grace, the appropriate medical aid is the Holy Spirit's conviction, and the cup is faith. The faith to receive the free grace of God isn't something we supply in the process of salvation. It's something we're given and motivated to use.

Most commentators also wisely point out that subjective faith, although distinguishable from objective faith, cannot be separated from it. Belief and trust, to be genuine, must be placed in something. Thus, in a real sense, subjective faith doesn't exist until it is placed in objective truth. Paul affirmed this when he said, "Faith comes from hearing, and hearing by the word of Christ" (Romans 10:17). John alluded to it when he said that the things he had written would give Christians assurance of their salvation (1 John 5:13). And Peter testified to it when he said that we receive faith by the righteousness of our God and Savior, Jesus Christ.

God-given subjective faith converts us when it believes and trusts in revealed objective truth about Jesus Christ. It changes us from condemned, hopeless sinners to redeemed children of God by responding to the true knowledge of God. It accepts and relies on the person and work of God's Son, by which our salvation has been fully accomplished.[3] It understands so as to appropriate that Jesus is God, that He is Savior, and that He is righteous.

Peter uses a single definite article in Greek to link "God and Savior," thus applying both terms to Jesus Christ.[4] This critical phrase emphasizes that salvation from sin required the incarnation of Christ because of God's righteousness. God is too pure to look upon evil (Habakkuk 2:13) and will not allow sin to go unpunished (Exodus 34:6–7). He cannot simply overlook sin and welcome His chosen children into His presence. In order to establish a family relationship with them, He had to send Jesus Christ to stand in their place. Jesus Christ was their substitute who fulfilled the demands of God's righteousness on their behalf.

Jesus' substitutionary atonement was necessary to fulfill the demands of God's righteousness. And, as the God-man, He was the only one who could do it. As God He was free from sin's taint and curse. And as man, He identified with fallen sinners while living in perfect conformity to God's holy law and paying our penalty for breaking that law. The righteousness of God the Son upheld the righteousness of God the Father in securing the salvation of His chosen children. We lay claim to that salvation when we exercise the subjective faith we've received to believe and trust in the truth we've been told.

The true knowledge of God, working in our salvation, blesses us with His grace and peace. Through no merit of our own, we freely receive His loving merciful pardon (Ephesians 2:8–9). And despite our natural animosity toward Him, our long war against God is brought to an end (Ephesians 5:8–10). We become new creations, God's beloved children. We are given new hearts of flesh to replace our hard hearts of stone and are called to walk worthy of our new identity.

Of course, we don't have any natural ability to fulfill that high calling. And if we did, we'd get the glory instead of God. So Peter tells us that the true knowledge of God continues to work in our sanctification, multiplying God's grace and peace to us so that God gets the glory for equipping us fully to live out our salvation.

> Grace and peace be multiplied to you in the knowledge of God and of Jesus our Lord; seeing that His divine power has granted to us everything pertaining to life and godliness through the true knowledge of Him who called us by His own glory and excellence. For by these He has granted to us His precious and magnificent promises, so that by them you might become partakers of the divine nature, having escaped the corruption that is in the world by lust. (2 Peter 1:2–4)

Grace and peace are not only the means of our salvation. They are also the means of our sanctification. Peter says they are multiplied in our lives as we grow in the true knowledge of God. As we study, learn, and apply God's revealed truth, His grace works in us to empower obedience. And as we tighten our grip on His precious promises, His peace permeates to the core of our beings.

Multiplied grace and peace glorify God by equipping us to walk worthy of our high calling. God puts His treasure in earthen vessels and calls us to work out our salvation in total reliance on Him. He does that so that "the surpassing greatness of the power" required for obedience obviously comes from Him instead of from us (2 Corinthians 4:7; Philippians 2:12–13). Thus the grace of obedience glorifies Him. God also commands us to cast all our anxiety on Him, asking Him to meet all our needs in His service. When we rely on those promises, we reflect incomprehensible peace to those around us (Philippians 4:6–7; 1 Peter 5:7). Our contentment and trust in His perfect care also glorify Him.

My friend Jennifer just found out she's pregnant with her fourth child. Good news, right? She's also forty-seven years old and has a thyroid condition requiring medication that, if she continues to take it, could harm the baby. Still good news? *"Yes!"* she says. Jennifer has a deep knowledge of God and an iron grip on His promises. She's well aware that the vessel in which God chose to place this new life is not only earthen but no longer young. But because she has been growing in grace and knowledge, she trusts God completely. She knows the road ahead may be festooned with potholes, but she also knows that God laid out the road and will walk it with her. Jennifer is relying on the surpassing greatness of God's power to fuel her obedience. She is letting Him carry all her anxiety. She is sure He will meet her every need in His service. My friend is reflecting incomprehensible peace in a situation many women would find supremely distressing. She is walking worthy of her high calling in Christ because her contentment and trust glorify God.

Although sanctification, unlike salvation, does require our most diligent effort, God fully equips, supports, and motivates the effort we make. His divine power provides all that we need for life and godliness. And His precious and magnificent promises sustain us as we live out our salvation in a dark, fallen world.

We appropriate the power and the promises through the true knowledge of God. His indwelling Spirit quickens the truth revealed in the Bible to give us spiritual life and empower us to pursue godly behavior. He works through God's promises to help us understand our indissoluble union with Christ, which equips us to resist the temptations of sin and tightens our grip on our sure inheritance. The Spirit, armed with the Word, glorifies God by transforming our minds and conforming us to the image of Christ.

The true knowledge of God not only generates life; it focuses life around God's purposes for it. It asserts, indicatively, that we are God's children, that we have been called out of the world to reflect His glory, that we possess irrefutable, glorious promises, and that we live in union with Christ. Then it commands, imperatively, that we use what we have been given to serve Christ wholeheartedly.

Peter goes on to say that when Christian service demands that we go to war against teachers of heresy, true knowledge of God will spur us to fight valiantly and assure us of victory.

True Knowledge Spurs and Assures
(2 Peter 1:5–11)

D. Martyn Lloyd-Jones, in a sermon on 2 Peter, makes the startling assertion that the gospel isn't interested in our behavior—until after we're saved. I don't know whether he paused for effect where I put the dash, but such a timely pause would have accented the critical point he was making: The gospel is not a call for us to be saved by doing something; it is a proclamation that we have been saved because something has been done for us. However, once we are saved, the gospel demands that we do a lot![5]

Peter has already explained the Good News of what's been done for us. And now he turns his attention to what we're to do in the light and the strength of what we've received. He says that the same knowledge of God that saved and equipped us to live out our salvation also spurs us to zealously serve God.

> Now for this very reason also, applying all diligence, in your faith supply moral excellence, and in your moral excellence, knowledge; and in your knowledge, self-control, and in your self-control, perseverance, and in your perseverance, godliness; and

171

in your godliness, brotherly kindness, and in your brotherly kindness, love. For if these qualities are yours and are increasing, they render you neither useless nor unfruitful in the true knowledge of our Lord Jesus Christ. For he who lacks these qualities is blind or short-sighted, having forgotten his purification from his former sins. (1:5–9)

Peter knew that the war on God's Word couldn't be won by self-centered, ease-conscious, half-hearted soldiers. So he commanded recruits to "apply all diligence" in using their God-given equipment. In other words, we are to eagerly exert ourselves, in full dependence on God, to lavishly add an abundance of Christlike character traits to the faith we've been given. Each of these traits is empowered by faith and effective in proclaiming, living out, and defending the truth of God's Word.

D. Edmond Hiebert explains that our "faith is the seedbed out of which Christian character grows. A vital orthodoxy [right belief and trust] produces a willing orthopraxy [right behavior]. Through daily exercise in moral living, faith attains its full potential in spiritual fruitfulness."[6]

Not only are these traits rooted in faith and effective for service, but also they seem to be inextricably interrelated.[7] Peter's wording suggests that each is, in some way, inherent in the ones that precede it; and that each is, in some way, enhanced by the ones that follow. He gives no hint that we're free to pick and choose traits to develop but exhorts us to deliberately (almost systematically) weave all of these traits into the fabric of our daily lives.

To the faith we've been given, we are to add moral excellence, or faithful obedience to God's commands driven by our desire to fulfill His purposes for our salvation. To our moral excellence, we are to add knowledge, or an increasing discernment between right and wrong in all our pursuits. To our knowledge, we are to add self-control, or an inner power to govern our desires and submit our energies to the cause of Christ.

To our self-control, we are to add perseverance, or endurance in difficult situations fueled by trust in God's promises and contentment in His care. To our perseverance, we are to add godliness, or a *Coram Deo*[8] perspective, a practical awareness of God in every aspect of life. To our godliness, we are to add brotherly kindness, a deep affection for our Christian siblings that willingly bears each other's burdens and persistently guards our family unity. And to our brotherly kindness, we are to add love, God's *agape,* which desires the highest good of those around us and acts self-sacrificially in their best interests.

Peter assures us that when we actively, consistently, and continually work at developing these character traits, we will be productive in service to God. We will not be lacking in spiritual sight, insight, or foresight[9] like those who reject or neglect God's demands on their lives. Rather, we will respond to the spur of the true knowledge of God and boldly proclaim, live out, and defend the truth of God's Word. In short, we will be valiant soldiers in the war on the Word.

But that's not all we will be. We will also be assured and confident of our standing in Christ and of the ultimate victory we'll share with Him. Peter says,

> Therefore, brethren, be all the more diligent to make certain about His calling and choosing you; for as long as you practice these things, you will never stumble; for in this way the entrance into the eternal kingdom of our Lord and Savior Jesus Christ will be abundantly supplied to you. (1:10–11)

When Peter told Christians to be diligent to make certain about God's calling and choosing[10] them, he was exhorting us to ground our assurance in the visible evidence of transformation in Christ. But he was not advocating some kind of checklist assurance that relies on accomplishment instead of mercy and grace. He was telling us we can know (for a fact, without doubt) that we are redeemed by looking at what God has done in our lives. Hiebert explains that "robust spiritual growth confirms that God has called and chosen us."[11] And Douglas J. Moo affirms that "one cannot be a true Christian without showing the effect of one's relationship with Christ in a renewed lifestyle."[12]

Assurance of our salvation recognizes that the same grace that brought us into God's family and equips us for service also keeps us secure[13] in our faith and leads us home in triumphant victory. Assurance of our salvation is based on God's divine power at work in our lives and on His precious and magnificent promises. Assurance is no flippant presumption that "once saved, always saved" means that we don't have to work hard at obeying our Lord. Nor is assurance a proud assumption that we can, by our efforts, cease to sin in this life. Rather, it is a Christ-confident, grace-dependent perspective of our purpose on earth and our reward in heaven, which is generated and fueled by true knowledge of God.

The assurance that flows from God's revelation exalts the work of our Lord Jesus Christ as it reflects the true nature of our salvation. Peter says we should be "all the more diligent" (v. 10) in our pursuit of assurance because it testifies clearly of God's glorious grace.

Notes

1. Commentators hotly debate the authorship of 2 Peter. I agree with those who maintain that the evidence for Peter's authorship is stronger and more reliable than

the evidence against it. See D. Edmond Hiebert, *Second Peter and Jude: An Expositional Commentary* (Greenville, S.C.: Unusual Publications, 1989), 1–20, for an excellent overview and analysis of this evidence. Douglas J. Moo also provides insightful support for Peter's authorship of 2 Peter in *The NIV Application Commentary: 2 Peter and Jude* (Grand Rapids: Zondervan, 1996).

2. The Greek word translated "received" in 2 Peter 1:1 is *lanchanō*. Kenneth Wuest defines it as "to obtain by lot, to receive by divine allotment," and goes on to explain that "the faith here is appropriating faith exercised by the believing sinner when he places his trust in the Lord Jesus. This faith is given in sovereign grace by God to the sinner elected (chosen out) to salvation, and is part of the salvation which is given him" (*Wuest's Word Studies from the Greek New Testament,* vol. 2, *Philippians, Hebrews, The Pastoral Epistles, First Peter, In These Last Days* [Grand Rapids: Eerdmans, 1973], 16). Simon J. Kistemaker, in his commentary on 2 Peter, says, "Peter uses this verb [received] to indicate that man receives his faith from God in accordance with God's will. He reminds his readers that faith does not originate in themselves, but is a gift from God" (*New Testament Commentary: Exposition of Peter* [Grand Rapids: Baker, 1996], 241).

3. Please keep in mind that our response to the work of Jesus Christ plays no part in the accomplishment of our salvation. Jesus Christ fully accomplished salvation for all of the elect in His life, death, resurrection, and ascension. Our response to what He has done, made possible by God's gift of faith, is the conversion experience that confirms to us that we have been saved and adopted as one of God's children. Although our salvation was assured by God before the foundation of the world and accomplished by

Christ on the cross, it becomes known to us when we receive and exercise the faith we have received.

4. Kistemaker, *Exposition of Peter*, 242.

5. D. M. Lloyd-Jones, *Expository Sermons on 2 Peter* (Carlisle, Pa.: Banner of Truth Trust, 1983), 23–24.

6. Hiebert, *Second Peter and Jude*, 52.

7. Here is an example of searching for truth "as for hidden treasures" (Proverbs 2:4). The interrelatedness of these character traits is not clearly evident when we first read the passage. In order to mine this rich gem of wisdom, we must dig it up through careful study of the individual words.

8. *Coram Deo* means "before God."

9. I borrowed this catchy phrase from Griffith Thomas: Robert Leighton and Griffith Thomas, *The Crossway Classic Commentaries: 1 and 2 Peter*, ed. Alister McGrath and J. I. Packer (Wheaton, Ill.: Crossway, 1999), 266.

10. Peter reverses the actual order of these events (calling and choosing) to clarify the point he is making. He is discussing the believer's assurance of salvation rather than God's eternal decree. Therefore, he describes the reality of salvation from the believer's perspective. Although election (choosing) precedes calling chronologically, we are aware of our calling before we understand that we have been chosen. Only after we respond to God's call are we able to accept and appreciate that we were chosen for salvation before the foundation of the world.

11. Hiebert, *Second Peter and Jude*, 59.

12. Moo, *2 Peter and Jude,* 47.

13. The distinction between assurance and security is important. Assurance is an attitude we can develop and maintain; security is a reality whether we believe it or not. We are secure in our salvation because God preserves us in it (2 Timothy 1:12). However, we may lack assurance of this reality for various reasons, which are usually related to neglect of spiritual disciplines or persistent, unrepentant sin in our lives.

Exercises

Review

1. Read the brief epistle of 2 Peter two or three times. Then explain in your own words how the phrase "war on the Word" summarizes it. Also explain the importance of heeding Peter's call to active duty in this war.

2. Describe the role of true knowledge of God in the conversion of sinners.

3. Distinguish between subjective and objective faith and explain how each is a gift of God's grace.

4. Describe the role of true knowledge of God in equipping God's children for service.

5. Explain, in your own words, D. Edmond Hiebert's statement: "A vital orthodoxy produces a willing orthopraxy."

6. List and define each of the character traits Peter tells us to diligently supply in our walk with the Lord. List some practical ways we can obey this command. Why is it important to obey this command?

7. How can we be certain that God has called and chosen us to be His children? Why is it important for us to be certain about this?

Application

1. Review your memory verses from the previous lesson. Then begin memorizing one or more of the following:

   Galatians 2:20
   2 Peter 1:3–4
   1 John 5:13

2. This week during your prayer times, use the true knowledge of God found in Galatians 2:20 and 2 Peter 1:3–4 to help you give thanks to God for the way He equips you to serve Him effectively. Also use Romans 8:31–39; Ephesians 4:14–32; and Philippians 2:13–14 to help you confess your failures and seek God's help to diligently build and maintain Christian character traits and pursue assurance of your salvation.

3. Review your answer to review exercise 6. Which of these character traits do you believe are clearly reflected in your daily life? Which ones do you believe are reflected only dimly? Consult with three or four close friends or relatives to see if they agree with your self-assessment. (If they don't, prayerfully consider revising your self-assessment!) Thank God in prayer for the grace that equips you to clearly reflect the traits that you do, and ask Him to help you continue reflecting them well. Then using a concordance and godly counsel from wise, knowledgeable mentors, seek out applicable Scripture passages that will help you strengthen your dim traits. Make a step-by-step plan for applying these passages

to your daily life, and enlist the aid of one or more people who love you enough to hold you accountable for following through on your plan. Check with those three or four close friends or relatives in a month or two to see if they notice any changes in you.

4. Do you possess assurance that you are saved? If so, on what are you basing your assurance? If not, what thoughts or beliefs are hindering you from having assurance? In either case, read and study Isaiah 43:1–13; John 10:27–30; 17:1–26; Romans 8:31–39; 2 Timothy 1:12; 1 Peter 1:1–5; 2:9–10; 2 Peter 1:1–11; and 1 John 5:13, 20. According to these verses, is it possible to have true assurance of your salvation? According to these verses, on what is true assurance based? According to these verses, why is it important to have true assurance? Has your view of assurance changed as a result of studying these verses? If so, explain.

Digging Deeper

1. Study Philippians 2:12–13 in light of what Peter teaches in 2 Peter 1:1–11, and then write a brief paragraph describing the relationship between God's equipping grace and our good works. How might you use this "true knowledge of God" to respond to someone who tells you, "God's grace means that I can do whatever I want"? How might you use it to respond to someone who tells you, "God saves us by grace, but we have to keep ourselves saved by doing good works"?

2. Read Psalm 106:21; Isaiah 43:3, 11; 45:15, 21; 49:26; 60:16; 63:7–8; Hosea 13:4; Colossians 2:9; and Hebrews 1:3. How do these passages support Peter's affirmation, in 2 Peter 1:1, that Jesus Christ is God?

Primary Passage
2 Peter 1:12–21

Supplementary Passages
Numbers 24:17
Psalm 119:105
Isaiah 42:1–4
Jeremiah 1:9
Matthew 17:1–8
Luke 9:28–36; 22:31–34
John 21:18–19
Romans 15:4, 15
1 Corinthians 2:9–16
2 Corinthians 11:13–15
Ephesians 2:19–22; 4:11–16
2 Timothy 1:6–2:14; 3
James 5:19–20
1 Peter 1:10–12
1 John 1:1–5; 2:21
Revelation 22:16

Before reading the lesson material, please read the primary Scripture passage listed above and as many of the supplementary passages as time allows. Then briefly summarize in your notebook what you have read. (Do not go into detail. Limit your summary to a brief description of the people, events, and/or ideas discussed in the passages.)

11

The Reminder of Scripture's Authority

It is a very great mistake to think that because we know a thing we need not be reminded of it repeatedly.
—D. Martyn Lloyd-Jones

Human beings are forgetful creatures. If you are anything like me (and you probably are), you depend on reminders to get through each day. I hate to think how many meetings, appointments, plans, intentions, commitments, and promises we would miss or ignore if something or someone didn't jog our memories continually.

The white board in my hallway is festooned with hurriedly scrawled notes like "call Diana," "clean the bathroom," and "pick up the dry cleaning." The ceiling-to-floor year-at-a-glance calendar in my husband's home office is not only marked up with his schedule and mine. It's also color-coded, so we can tell whose schedule is whose. I carry a Day-Timer, slap sticky notes on the mirror, and pile up right by the door everything I need to take with me when I leave the house. The mail I pulled out of the box yesterday included reminders that my Discover Card payment is due April 3, that a friend's baby shower is fast approaching, that the DAV is picking up useful discards next Tuesday, and that it's time for my dog to make her yearly trek to the vet.

Where would I be without all those reminders? Most assuredly frustrated, confused, stressed out, and embarrassed. And probably a lot more irresponsible, unreliable, and inconsiderate. All those reminders help me look out not only for my interests but also for the interests of others. They shore up the forgetfulness of my fallen mind, bring a semblance of order to my chaotic life, and effectuate my desires to be conscientious, dependable, and thoughtful of others.

One of the things I find most fascinating about reminders is that they rarely provide any new information. The notes on my white board aren't news to me. Nor are the events color-coded on my husband's calendar, the entries in my Day-Timer, the words on those sticky notes, or that ever-present pile of stuff by the door. I know that my Discover Card payment is due at the first of the month, that my friend's baby shower is being planned, that the DAV picks up useful discards every so often, and that my dog sees her vet (who is aptly named Dr. Schott) at least once a year.

However, knowing those things doesn't assure that I'll take appropriate action at the right time. Unless I'm reminded frequently of what I know, I'm inclined not to act on what I know when I should. And such failure to act can produce some unhappy consequences ranging from slightly disturbing to decidedly serious. Not calling Diana may put a slight strain on our friendship, but not taking my dog to the vet could threaten her life. Because human beings (like you and me) are forgetful creatures, we need reminders if we want to live well in this world.

It would be nice if salvation in Christ cured our forgetfulness, but it doesn't. Redeemed, transformed sinners are just as forgetful as their lost fellow humans. Therefore we should not be surprised by the constant reminders we find in the Bible. They are there because forgetting to heed God's revealed truth has eternal consequences far more significant than forgetting to pay a credit card bill. The disciples of Christ who wrote the New Testament understood that their task encompassed a good deal of reminding. They knew they had been called not only to teach and proclaim the news of the gospel to those ignorant of it. They had also been called to remind those to whom it was no longer news to remember and act on it.

Paul wasn't shy about reminding Timothy to "kindle afresh the gift of God which is in you," to "retain the standard of sound words which you have heard from me," to "guard . . . the treasure which has been entrusted to you," and to pass on "the things which you heard from me . . . to faithful men who will . . . teach others also" (2 Timothy 1:6, 13–14; 2:2).

James encouraged his brethren to turn straying sinners back to the truth they were ignoring (James 5:19–20). John admonished believers who "do know" the truth to walk in the light of it (1 John 1:5–7; 2:21). Jude, out of "desire to remind" believers to act on the truth that they know, exhorted them to "contend earnestly for" and build themselves up in the faith, to hold fast to the love of God, and to have mercy on others (vv. 3–5, 20–23).

And Peter, in this section of his second epistle, reminds "those who have received a faith of the same kind as ours" (1:1) to "call to mind" (1:15) what they know about God's revealed truth as they engage false teachers in the war on God's Word.

You Must Remember This
(2 Peter 1:12–15)

Peter wrote to believers under attack. In his first letter, he affirmed the sufficiency of their spiritual resources to respond to persecution in such a way that God gets the glory. He told believers who suffer at the hands of ungodly sinners to stand firm in God's grace and thereby foil Satan's desire to blur the display of God's glory in our fallen world.

Peter knew, from experience, that personal assault has a way of shifting our focus from the things above to the things of this world. He knew, from experience, how severely we're tempted to trade exaltation of God for protection of self when we're threatened with harm. And he also knew, from experience, that God's grace alone is sufficient to strengthen us to stand firm when our faith makes us targets of painful abuse.

But Peter knew that not all attacks against Christians come from outside their assemblies. He knew that God's enemy, Satan, is just as devious as he is vicious. Not content to limit the battle to well-defined fields, he disguises himself as a brother, infiltrates Christian fellowship, and attacks from within. This kind of attack is very dangerous because it is not only insidious but painless at first. Deception is sneaky, but it doesn't hurt right away. It feigns friendship while concealing malevolence in warm embraces. It takes advantage of family trust while spreading disease through close personal relationships. It plays its role well while fostering complacency. Deception is dangerous because it doesn't announce its intentions or assault us directly. Defending against it is hard because we don't see it coming.

My daughter was involved in a serious car accident a few months ago. She was proceeding through an intersection (with the green light) next to a minivan when a small car ran the red light at a high rate of speed. The small car smashed into the minivan with enough force to flip it into the air. It slammed down on Cinnamon's car, destroying the front left side, including the driver's door. By God's grace, she was not seriously injured. But she was thoroughly shaken by her total helplessness. "Mom," she said, later that evening. "I heard a crash and looked up to see a minivan coming down out of the sky." There was literally nothing she could do to defend herself because she didn't see what was coming. She got blind-sided, which is exactly how false teachers attack Christians in churches.

Deception within the body of Christ was a big problem in the first century, and it's a big problem today. False teachers have run loose in the church, and still do, for at least two reasons: they are quite good at hiding their wolfishness under sheep's clothing; and we are quite prone to forget the truth that we know. False teachers almost never show up at the church door and announce, "Hello, orthodox Christians. I am here to pervert and twist God's revelation little by little until I succeed in convincing you to believe Satan's lies." Rather, they pass themselves off as genuine Christians and prey on our forgetfulness to lead us astray.

Peter, a devoted apostle who deeply loved those the Lord had committed into his care, knew that false teachers posed a grave threat to his flock. So he wrote to exhort endangered believers not to be duped by the cunning wiles of such teachers. Although Christian hospitality could well invite a disguised wolf into the fold, Christian forgetfulness should not accede to his teaching.

Peter knew that his readers were fully equipped to unmask the false sheep among them. They had at their disposal the essential weapon in the war on God's Word—the sword of the Spirit, which is true knowledge of God. But Peter also knew that believers were prone to forget where they put that weapon. His deep concern for their eternal well-being rings clear in his charge to keep the sword nearby and well honed for use.

> Therefore, I will always be ready to remind you of these things, even though you already know them,

and have been established in the truth which is present with you. And I consider it right, as long as I am in this earthly dwelling, to stir you up by way of reminder, knowing that the laying aside of my earthly dwelling is imminent, as also our Lord Jesus Christ has made clear to me. And I will also be diligent that at any time after my departure you will be able to call these things to mind. (1:12–15)

We can infer from these words that at the time Peter wrote them, he was an old man looking death square in the face. And if his words were written, as many believe, during the reign of the Roman emperor Nero, we can be sure that the face on which he was gazing was a far cry from pretty. Jesus had told Peter that he would die as an old man in a violent manner (John 21:18–19). And Peter seems sure that his prophesied end is at hand. However, he does not appear to be all that concerned about how he will die.

Peter's concern, at this juncture, is that he is short of time to minister to those under his care. Imminent death has a way of clarifying priorities. So we can be sure that the things on Peter's mind when he wrote this letter were of the utmost importance to him. Matthew Henry captures the old apostle's consuming mindset when he says that "the nearness of death makes the apostle diligent in the business of life."[1]

Peter's "business of life" had been defined by his Lord Jesus Christ on the eve of His crucifixion and Peter's great failure. Jesus had bluntly predicted Peter's denial and then just as bluntly described the life's work to which God had called him. "Simon, Simon," He said. "Behold, Satan has demanded permission to sift you like wheat; but I have prayed for you that your faith may not fail; and you, when once you have turned again, strengthen your brothers" (Luke 22:31–32).

Peter's apostolic commission to "follow Jesus" (John 21:19–23) had been a mandate to strengthen believers—and he had precious little time left in which to do that. So he told them that they must remember the truth in which, by God's grace, they had been established.[2] Peter knew and would go on to describe the dangerous threat posed by false teachers infiltrating the body. But he did not give his readers a lot of new information about how to fight them. Instead, he reminded them to hold on to what they already knew.

Peter used the short time he had left to equip believers to valiantly fight the war on God's Word in full assurance of ultimate victory. He did that by stirring them up by way of reminder to strengthen their grip on the sword of the Spirit. True knowledge of God was, and still is, the essential weapon in the war on the Word because it was, and still is, absolutely invincible. All of God's foes must yield eventually to its authority.

The Truth Is Still the Truth
(2 Peter 1:16–21)

However, not all of God's foes yield immediately to Scripture's authority. Some delay the inevitable for as long as possible. Their leader, Satan, is well aware that the war has been won in the triumph of Christ, but his intense hatred for God drives him to keep fighting for as long as he can. He's not the least bit inclined to lay down his weapons or sign a peace treaty.

Rather, he seeks to inflict as much damage as possible before being forced into abject surrender. He turns up the heat on believers by launching a two-pronged attack. He dispatches some of his minions to fiercely assault God's people from outside their churches. And he instructs others to cunningly infiltrate Christian ranks from inside those churches.

Both assault forces know they can't defeat the sword of the Spirit, so they target our grip and try to disarm us. The outside assault force takes aim directly. It instills fear and inflicts pain in an effort to knock the sword from our hands. The inside assault force is much more subtle, however. It slyly entices us to lay the sword down voluntarily.

Peter's first letter was written to equip believers to fight outside assault. He gave us the weapons of hope and encouragement and told us to "stand firm" in the true grace of God. Now Peter writes to equip us to fight sneaky infiltrators. He says we must grow in God's grace and in the knowledge of Jesus Christ if we want to unmask and defeat the false teachers among us.

False teachers come in two basic varieties: those who teach blatant lies and those who dish out deception. True believers in Christ are seldom seduced by obvious liars. But they are, far too often, led astray by deceivers. That's because artful deception sounds a lot like the truth. Those who dispense it are adept at hiding their lies behind a scriptural façade, redefining significant biblical words, and distorting theology with irresponsible proof texting. Deceptive false teachers use just enough truth to lull Christians into a false sense of security. And then they prey on our tendency to forget what we know to slowly lead us away from the full counsel of God.

When we succumb to the false teachers' devices, we fail to grow in God's grace and the knowledge of Jesus Christ. And failure to grow relaxes our grip on the sword of the Spirit. Peter says it might slip right out of our hands if we fail to heed his earnest warning. He says that false teachers succeed, in large measure, by systematically sabotaging God-given authority. They begin by undermining the authority of those God has called to proclaim His truth and end by disavowing the authority of God's Word itself.

Peter implies that he had been falsely accused of teaching "cleverly devised tales" (1:16). And he wasn't alone. Paul's defense of his ministry to the Corinthians suggests that he had been similarly slandered (2 Corinthians 11:1–30). And John states quite clearly that he had been too (3 John 9–10). At this point in his letter, Peter shifts pronouns from "I" to "we," thus joining hands with his fellow maligned apostles to affirm that their teaching is no made-up myth.

> For we did not follow cleverly devised tales when we made known to you the power and coming of our Lord Jesus Christ, but we were eyewitnesses of His majesty. For when He received honor and glory from God the Father, such an utterance as this was made to Him by the Majestic Glory, "This is My beloved Son with whom I am well-pleased"—and we ourselves heard this utterance made from heaven when we were with Him on the holy mountain. So we have the prophetic word made more sure, to which you do well to pay attention as to a lamp shining in a dark place, until the day dawns and the morning star arises in your hearts. But know this first of all, that no prophecy of Scripture is a matter of one's own interpretation, for no prophecy was ever made by an act of human will, but men moved by the Holy Spirit spoke from God. (2 Peter 1:16–21)

Peter obviously realized that some of his flock would be wondering, *Why should we trust you instead of these other teachers? How do we know you're right about them and they're wrong about you?* He anticipated and dealt with those legitimate questions by affirming his apostolic authority to speak from God. Authority is a relational concept that gives certain persons or entities the right to command and expect compliance from others. Absolute authority is held only by God, but He delegates other forms of authority to those He calls to perform certain tasks.

When God revealed His truth to humanity, He used a divine process called inspiration. He chose certain men, known as prophets and apostles, to record His Word under the empowering influence of His Holy Spirit. These men spoke with authority because they were divinely enabled to speak and write God's infallible, inerrant, sufficient truth. They did not expound their own ideas about God that could (and most likely would) be subject to later revision. Rather, they were moved by the Spirit to speak truth from God. Thus, what they wrote was inspired revelation invested with the absolute authority held only by God. It commanded obedience and allowed no possibility of later revision.[3]

Peter was trustworthy because he was one of the men God had invested with apostolic authority. In this passage, he reminds his readers that the message proclaimed by the apostles did not have its source in their imaginations. They testified of actual events they had witnessed—events that indisputably fulfilled ancient biblical prophecies.

Peter had seen the glory of Christ's deity revealed in His transfiguration and heard God honor Him by audibly owning Him as His beloved Son in whom He was well pleased (Matthew 17:1–8; Mark 9:2–8; Luke 9:28–36). Many centuries before, men moved by the Spirit had spoken from God and predicted the coming of the Messiah. Peter saw the fulfillment of that inspired promise on "the holy mountain" and was also moved by the Spirit to speak from God about his experience.

Douglas J. Moo highlights the authority of the apostles and prophets when he notes that "the words Peter and the other apostles heard from heaven at the Transfiguration and the words that the prophets spoke came from the same place: God Himself."[4] And Dick Lucas and Christopher

Green underscore the authority of the Bible's whole message by saying, "The prophets were gripped by God as he spoke to them and gave them a message to communicate, and the New Testament writers unambiguously and consistently supported the prophets' claims."[5]

Peter says that his readers would do well to pay attention to the prophetic word "made more sure" (2 Peter 1:19) by the apostles' testimony. But by that he does not mean that the prophetic word was somehow unsure before apostolic experience confirmed it. The prophets who spoke from God spoke just as surely as did the apostles. Their words do not need apostolic verification in order to be accepted as true and trustworthy.

So how does the apostolic witness make the prophetic word more sure? Simply put, by bolstering our confidence in the fact that God keeps His word. D. Martyn Lloyd-Jones said that fulfilled prophecy "is a great declaration of the immutability of the counsel of God, that God's word is fixed and absolute and eternal."[6] The apostolic testimony confirming the fulfillment of prophetic promises of the coming of Jesus lays down the strongest possible foundation for God's church in the world (Ephesians 2:19–22). It allows us to stand firmly on full revelation. We don't have to fight nagging doubts about whether God can and will do what He says. Because we have been blessed to be born and reborn on this side of the cross, we know, for a fact, without doubt, that God keeps His word.

That assurance functions as "a lamp shining in a dark place" (2 Peter 1:19) to encourage us to tighten our grip on the sword of the Spirit. As we grow in God's grace and the knowledge of Jesus Christ, we'll be less likely to fall prey to the tactics of deceptive false teachers who run loose in the church. Instead, we'll wield the sword to unmask and defeat them and foil Satan's desire to blur the display of God's glory in our dark, fallen world.

Notes

1. Quoted in Michael Bentley, *Living for Christ in a Pagan World: 1 and 2 Peter Simply Explained,* The Welwyn Commentary Series (Durham, England: Evangelical Press, 1990), 200.

2. The Greek word translated "established" means "to make stable, place firmly, set fast" (Kenneth S. Wuest, *Wuest's Word Studies from the Greek New Testament,* vol. 2, *Philippians, Hebrews, The Pastoral Epistles, First Peter, In These Last Days* [Grand Rapids: Eerdmans, 1973], 28). Peter said that the believers to whom he wrote were mature and stable in their faith because they knew God's truth. But he also warned them of how quickly their stability could be shaken if they forgot and/or failed to act on what they knew.

3. Commentators disagree about whether 2 Peter 1:20 should be understood as referring to the recording of Scripture by the original writers or the understanding of Scripture by those who read it. I agree with those who hold that the context of the verse supports the first option better than the second, and I have written this section with that interpretation in mind. Gordon Clark states the case well when he says that 2 Peter 1:21 explains (gives the logical reason for) 2 Peter 1:20; therefore, verse 20 is saying that scriptural prophecy did not result from the will of the writers but from the will of God. "Isaiah did not get out of bed one morning and say, I have decided to write some prophesies today," Clark explains. "God picked Isaiah up and carried him along; and, so supported, Isaiah spoke words from God" (*New Heavens, New Earth: A Commentary on First and Second Peter* [Jefferson, Md.: The Trinity Foundation, 1967, 1972, 1993], 192). For a clear presentation of the other argu-

ment, see J. N. D. Kelly, *Black's New Testament Commentaries: The Epistles of Peter and Jude,* ed. Henry Chadwick (London: A&C Black, 1969; Peabody, Mass.: Hendrickson, 1969), 324.

4. Douglas J. Moo, *The NIV Application Commentary: 2 Peter and Jude* (Grand Rapids: Zondervan, 1996), 79.

5. Dick Lucas and Christopher Green, *The Bible Speaks Today: The Message of 2 Peter and Jude,* ed. John R. W. Stott (Downers Grove, Ill.: InterVarsity Press, 1995), 83.

6. D. M. Lloyd-Jones, *Expository Sermons on 2 Peter* (Carlisle, Pa.: Banner of Truth Trust, 1983), 88.

Exercises

Review

1. Explain the importance of frequent reminders in our daily lives. If you have access to a concordance, look up the words *remember, remembrance, remind, reminded,* and *reminder.* Read a broad sampling of verses in which these words occur and briefly explain the necessity of remembering biblical truth.

2. Describe the particular danger of the inside attack launched by false teachers against the church. How does Peter say we should arm ourselves against this kind of attack?

3. Read Luke 22:24–34 and John 21:15–23. How is Peter's commission to strengthen his brethren and tend Jesus' sheep reflected in his exhortation to believers recorded in 2 Peter 1:12–15?

4. Describe the two basic varieties of false teachers. Which variety poses the greater threat to believers who are established in the truth? How do these false teachers usually succeed?

5. Define "authority." Carefully read 2 Peter 1:16–21; then support, in your own words, Christianity's claim that the Bible is inherently and absolutely authoritative. How does the Bible's authority relate to its use as the sword of the Spirit? (For a little more insight, see Ephesians 6:10–20.)

6. How is the prophetic word made more sure by the apostles' testimony?

Application

1. Review your memory verses from the previous lesson. Then begin memorizing one or more of the following:

   Psalm 119:105
   Romans 15:4
   2 Timothy 3:14–17

2. This week during your prayer times, use 1 Peter 1:1–9 and 2 Peter 1:1–11 to help you strengthen your grip on the sword of the Spirit by remembering the undeniable truth of the gospel in which you have been established.

3. Think hard, be creative, and list many practical ways in which you can systematically remind yourself of the truths in which you have been established (for example, daily Bible reading, Scripture memory, listening to sermon tapes, hanging embroidered Scripture passages on the wall). Which of these are you currently practic-

ing? Pick one or two that you are not currently practicing and make a specific, step-by-step plan that will help you begin this week to practice them.

4. Is Scripture *practically* authoritative in your life? Do you routinely make decisions based on identifiable biblical principles? Do you pattern your thoughts, words, and actions after biblical examples? Do you consistently view all situations of life from a biblical perspective? Do you habitually reach for your Bible when someone asks you for advice or when you start to pray? If you answered yes to any or all of the above questions, give one or more specific examples in support of each yes. If you answered no to one or more of the questions, how does Peter's exhortation and his example in this lesson motivate you to live more fully under Scripture's authority? How might your answers to application exercise 3 help you implement your desire to live more fully under Scripture's authority?

Digging Deeper

1. Michael Bentley, in his commentary on 1 and 2 Peter, refers to a group of atheists and agnostics who campaign to have Bibles removed from hotel rooms. Then he says, "We might feel sad that this group of people wanted Bibles removed from certain hotel rooms, but the question we should ask ourselves about this story is, 'Do atheists and agnostics recognize the power of God's Word more than we do?' " (Michael Bentley, *Living for Christ in a Pagan World: 1 and 2 Peter Simply Explained,* The Welwyn Commentary Series [Durham, England: Evangelical Press, 1990], 203). Reflect on Bentley's question, and then answer it in light of what you have learned so far in this study.

2. What does Peter's primary concern as he faces death tell you about his perspective on Christian living? (Hint: Think about how Peter's pursuit of his business of life as he nears death reflects his grace-conscious, grace-filled, and grace-dependent approach to life in general. It may help to review the introduction and lesson 1 of this study if you need help making this connection.)

Primary Passage
2 Peter 2

Supplementary Passages
Genesis 6:1–9:17; 13:1–13; 18–19
Numbers 22–24
Deuteronomy 13:1–5; 18:20–22
Proverbs 26:11
Jeremiah 14:14–16; 23:1, 16, 25–32
Ezekiel 13:3–16
Matthew 7:22–23; 24:5–28
Luke 17:26–29
John 8:34
Acts 20:17–32
Romans 1:18–32
Ephesians 4:11–16
1 Timothy 6:3–5
2 Timothy 3
Hebrews 11:7
1 John 4:1
2 John 9–10
Jude

Before reading the lesson material, please read the primary Scrip-ture passage listed above and as many of the supplementary passages as time allows. Then briefly summarize in your note-book what you have read. Do not go into detail. Limit your sum-mary to a brief description of the people, events, and/or ideas discussed in the passages.

12

The Danger of
Twisted Teaching

*There are wolves out there who will devour the sheep.
And there are times when we have to take them on.*

—R. C. Sproul

Did R. C. Sproul's words introducing this lesson make you uncomfortable? If so, you're not alone. That's how they affected me when I heard them at the 2002 Ligonier Conference. I know that wolves infiltrate God's flock. I even know who a few of them are. But I don't want any part of "taking them on." I'd rather leave that to guys like R. C. And you probably would too!

But the fact is we can't. Active duty in the war on God's Word demands that we not only be able to speak the truth in love. We must also be able to recognize error and stand firm against it. But does that mean that everyone with whom we disagree should be taken on as a wolf? Absolutely not, said R. C. Sproul.

Speaking on the subject of "Brothers in Arms," he affirmed that there is a big difference between honest doctrinal differences and wolfish false teaching. And he wisely warned us to avoid two extremes when we disagree about doctrine: "Going to the mat" on every issue, no matter how minor; and refusing to "go to the mat" on any issue, no matter how major. Both extremes discredit the witness of God's church in the world and weaken our efforts to fulfill our chief end. We do not glorify God by contentiously breaking fellowship over every vague issue or by patiently tolerating what God says is intolerable.

R. C. affirmed what Peter teaches in his second epistle: We can preserve the unity of the Spirit in the bond of peace without tolerating the intolerable by submitting our disagreements to Scripture's authority. When our opponents are willing to submit their minds, hearts, and lives to biblical truth, we should relate to them as brothers and sisters, even as we disagree about what Scripture teaches. However, when our opponents refuse to submit to Scripture's authority, we should relate to them as wolves bent on devouring the sheep.

Jesus warned His apostles about "false prophets, who come to you in sheep's clothing, but inwardly are ravenous wolves" (Matthew 7:15). He said His apostles would know them "by their fruits" (v. 16), and should "see to it" that they were not misled (Matthew 24:4). His apostles took His warning seriously and responsibly passed it along to those they taught.

Paul told the Galatians that anyone who preached a gospel contrary to what they had received from Christ Jesus was to be "accursed" (Galatians 1:8–9). He warned the Ephesian elders to be on guard against "savage wolves" who speak "perverse things" to draw Christians away from righteous obedience (Acts 20:27–32). He told the Philippians to "beware of the dogs, . . . evil workers, . . . and the false circumcision" (Philippians 3:2). And he exhorted his protégé, Timothy, to "instruct certain men not to teach strange

doctrines" and to be alert to and on guard against the proliferation of false teaching "in the last days" (1 Timothy
1:3–7; 2 Timothy 3:1–9).

John told believers not to believe every spirit but to test
the spirits to see whether they are from God, "because
many false prophets have gone out into the world" (1 John
4:1). He also affirmed that anyone who does not abide in
the teaching of Christ should not be received and greeted
as a brother (2 John 9–11). Jude warned about ungodly persons who creep into churches unnoticed and "turn the
grace of our God into licentiousness and deny our only
Master and Lord, Jesus Christ" (Jude 4).[1]

And Peter, with characteristic outspokenness, devoted a
third of his second letter to describing false teachers in
graphic detail. As we study these verses, we'll see that he
wanted believers to see through their deception to their
real agenda. We'll see that he wanted us to discern their
arrogant, self-exalting disdain for God and His Word. We'll
see that he wanted us to inspect their fruit, detect the un-
mistakable odor of putridness, and realize that ingesting it
would prove injurious to the spiritual health of the church.
And we'll see that he wanted us to take them on.

If that makes you uncomfortable, you're not alone. But
let's not allow our shared discomfort to distract us from fulfilling our chief end in this world. Let's join hands and remind one other that growing in grace and knowledge of
Jesus Christ equips us abundantly to do the good deeds that
glorify Him, even when we're way out of our comfort zones.

Who Are All These False Teachers, and Why Are They in My Church?
(2 Peter 2:1–10a)

Peter devoted the first chapter of his second epistle to equipping his readers to take on false teachers. He reminded

them that the sword of the Spirit, true knowledge of God, is the essential weapon in the war on God's Word. And he encouraged them to remember that this essential weapon is nothing short of invincible because it is forged of God's precious and magnificent promises.

Those promises not only assure redeemed children of God that His divine power has granted them "everything pertaining to life and godliness" (1:3). They equip them to "make certain about His calling and choosing [them]" (1:10). And they "abundantly supply" to them "the entrance into the eternal kingdom of our Lord and Savior Jesus Christ" (1:11). Peter wanted his readers not to forget that they could wield the sword of the Spirit in absolute confidence because it would surely accomplish God's ultimate purposes.

Peter stirred them up by way of reminder that God's revealed truth could be thoroughly trusted and that they would "do well to pay attention" to it. They had "the prophetic word made more sure" by the eyewitness accounts of apostles who had seen and heard God keep His word. Peter declared that his readers should "know first of all" that apostolic/prophetic teaching was invested with supreme authority. What they said didn't come from their imaginations or will. Instead they were "men moved by the Holy Spirit" who "spoke from God" (1:19–21).

Peter knew that we need to strengthen our grip on the sword of the Spirit because Satan's minions have wormed their way into our churches. They hate God so much that they fight on in full knowledge that the war has been won in the triumph of Christ. They are determined to inflict as much damage as possible until forced into abject surrender.

Since they know they can't defeat our invincible sword, they target our grip and try to disarm us. Unlike outside persecutors, inside infiltrators don't attack with brute force. Instead they use cunning deception to persuade us to lay down the sword voluntarily. Peter says they've been at it for centuries, their tactics don't change, and their doom is certain.

> But false prophets also arose among the people, just as there will also be false teachers among you, who will secretly introduce destructive heresies, even denying the Master who bought them, bringing swift destruction upon themselves. And many will follow their sensuality, and because of them the way of truth will be maligned; and in their greed they will exploit you with false words; their judgment from long ago is not idle, and their destruction is not asleep. (2:1–3)

Peter says that the false teachers who have plagued Christians throughout the past twenty centuries are not all that different from the false prophets who preyed upon God's people, Israel, during Old Testament times. Not only are they devious, self-willed, and greedy. But most importantly, they are doomed to destruction.

False teachers have not been gifted and called by God's Spirit to proclaim His truth to His people. Instead they deliver a message of their own devising on their own authority. They are not the least bit up front about their agenda. They disguise themselves as "blood-bought" believers and proceed to teach what God says is intolerable.[2] Christopher Green says, "What these men teach is not a permissible variant of the gospel. It is a range of 'damnable heresies' . . . which led straight to judgment."[3]

False teachers tend to be very popular because they preach the license of indulgence instead of the liberty of obedience. They flatter people instead of calling them to faithful repentance and encourage them to pursue fleshly pleasures instead of discipleship. It's no wonder they pack out large auditoriums and rack up donations. But false teachers don't have their followers' best interests at heart. They don't serve them in love; they manipulate them to fulfill their own selfish desires. D. Edmond Hiebert says that these teachers skillfully use "their contrived arguments as counterfeit coinage to make a profitable bargain."[4]

They may think they are serving themselves and pulling one over on God. But Peter says they are, in reality, servants of Satan and will not get away with what they are doing. Although their devices may temporarily malign "the way of truth" (2:2), they have already been judged and will eventually pay the price of destruction. Peter gives three examples of how God has dealt with folks like these in the past and encourages us in the process by affirming the powerful grace of His sovereign care.

Peter says, "God did not spare angels when they sinned, but cast them into hell and committed them to pits of darkness, reserved for judgment" (2:4). Although there's no consensus among reputable commentators about who these angels are, what they did, or where they are now, Peter's point is clear. No one is exempt from God's judgment on sin, and even though God's judgment may be delayed, it is nonetheless certain.

After affirming the sure evenhandedness of God's righteous judgment, Peter then comforts Christians by reassuring us of God's sovereign care. He reminds us that God preserved Noah with seven others "when He brought a flood upon the world of the ungodly." And "He rescued righteous Lot" when He "condemned the cities of Sodom and Gomorrah to destruction by reducing them to ashes."

Peter says that we don't have to fear that God might overlook a few of His own when He rains righteous punishment on ungodly sinners. The examples Peter cited affirm his conclusion that "the Lord knows how to rescue the godly from temptation, and to keep the unrighteous under punishment for the day of judgment" (2:9). But does that mean that Christians should expect to walk through this world in some kind of supernatural asbestos bubble? Does it mean that true believers should always escape unscathed from catastrophic disasters? Does it mean that His children never get slandered and abused, lose all their worldly possessions, come down with cancer, or die in plane crashes? No, it does not. It means that God can, and does, deliver us from disaster when He so chooses. But it's no guarantee that He'll always so choose. My daughter was spared serious injury in a terrible car crash. D. J.'s daughter was killed.

Notice the wording of Peter's assurance. He doesn't say that the Lord will rescue us from all difficulty. Peter says the Lord knows how to rescue the godly "from temptation" (v. 9). The word translated "temptation" is *peirasmos* in Greek. It is also translated by the English word *trial* in many places in Scripture. A *peirasmos* is a difficult circumstance that can be either a temptation to sin or an opportunity to glorify God, depending largely on how we respond to it.

Peter's words here echo Paul's in 1 Corinthians 10:12–13: "Therefore let him who thinks he stands take heed that he does not fall. No temptation [*peirasmos*] has overtaken you but such as is common to man; and God is faithful, who will not allow you to be tempted beyond what you are able, but with the temptation will provide the way of escape also, so that you may be able to endure it." And Peter's words also echo this exhortation from James: "Consider it all joy, my brethren, when you encounter various trials [*peirasmois*], knowing that the testing of your faith produces endurance" (James 1:2–3).

Peter is not guaranteeing us absolute insulation from all of life's difficulties. He is reminding us that God's grace equips us to fulfill our chief end of giving God glory as we respond to difficulties He has ordained. God knows precisely what each of His children can endure in the strength He provides; and He orders our circumstances accordingly for our good and His glory. Michael Green said it well: "Christianity is no insurance policy against the trials of life. God allows them to befall the Christian; he meets us in them and delivers us out of them. . . . The God of grace can be relied on."[5]

God's sovereign care is comforting and encouraging, but it is no license to drift to the sidelines and coast into heaven. False teachers who "indulge the flesh" and "despise authority" (2 Peter 2:10) know that although they can't steal our sure inheritance, they can blur the display of God's glory here and now. And they are determined to do so. If we want to fulfill our chief end in this world, we need to beat them, not join them, in that endeavor.

Beat Them; Don't Join Them
(2 Peter 2:10b–22)

I don't know any Christians who would knowingly join with false teachers in blurring God's glory. But I know of several who have done so unwittingly. A former pastor of mine spent a few months in a cult when he was new Christian. When my daughter was in high school, many of her friends were attracted to the radical prosperity gospel that distorts the clear teaching of Scripture. And a member of the church I now attend recently left our small fellowship to follow the false doctrine taught by a popular radio wolf.

Although I don't know the hearts of any of these folks, I believe most of them to be genuine Christians who were, for a time, deceived by false teachers. My former pastor repudiated the cult within a short time, and several of my daughter's friends now see the flaws in the prosperity gospel. Others of my daughter's friends and our straying church member, however, still cause me to wonder about their salvation.

Jesus said,

Not everyone who says to Me "Lord, Lord," will enter the kingdom of heaven, but he who does the will of My Father who is heaven will enter. Many will say to Me on that day, "Lord, Lord, did we not prophesy in Your name, and in Your name cast out demons, and in Your name perform many miracles?" And then I will declare to them, "I never knew you; depart from Me, you who practice lawlessness." (Matthew 7:21–23)

Frankly, those should be some of the most frightening words in all of Scripture. So if they didn't scare you, go back and read them again. They tell us it's possible to think we're Christians when we are not. They tell us it's possible to anticipate checking in to Christ's mansion in glory, only to find out, too late, that we don't have a room. They tell us it's possible to hear the One we've called Lord say, "I never knew you."

So what does that do to our assurance? Does it mean that we can't know for sure in this life that we are saved? No, it does not. Look carefully at Jesus' words. He clearly states that He will repudiate those "who practice lawlessness" and that He will receive those who do the will of His Father. We can know, most assuredly, which of those camps we're in by examining our attitude toward God and His Word. Douglas J. Moo says, "The litmus test of our Christianity is not how much we know but the degree to which what we know affects our attitudes and behavior."[6] Those who practice lawlessness despise God's authority, whereas those who do the will of the Father submit themselves to His truth.

Genuine Christians can be deceived for a time, particularly when they are new in the faith or not firmly grounded in Scripture. However, their redeemed attitude of submission makes them responsive to God's Holy Spirit working through His Word. That attitude, sooner or later, will break the grip of deceptive false teaching and lead them back to orthodox truth.

But that doesn't mean that believers shouldn't worry about being deceived. For when we fall for deception, we aid and abet God's enemy Satan. Following false teachers helps Satan blur the glory of God. When we do that, we fail to walk worthy of our high calling in Christ. So how do we guard against being deceived? By strengthening our grip on the sword of the Spirit. The more we grow in grace and knowledge of Jesus Christ, the more equipped we will be to recognize error and stand firm against it.

I recently spent a few days in Bozeman, Montana, where I stayed with a family who raises wheat, cattle, and chickens. One night after dinner, my hostess told me to bundle up. We were going down the road to move some chickens from one coop to another. It was quite dark outside and bitterly cold, so this city-girl from the warm desert asked her if it wouldn't be better to do that tomorrow—in the afternoon, when the temperature was above 0 degrees. My hostess said, "Absolutely not." And then went on to explain that chickens can't see at night and are therefore quite docile and easy to move. But in the daylight when they can see, they would fight us like crazy. She was right. Those "blind chickens" came along quietly and didn't give us a bit of trouble.

They make an apt illustration of the way false teachers move believers away from God's truth. They target the ones who don't see very well because they lack the light of deep knowledge of Scripture. False teachers know that "blind chicken" Christians are very cooperative, whereas "full-sighted" Christians will fight them like crazy. Friends, I know which kind of Christian I want to be. And I certainly hope you do too!

Peter says that false teachers are not hard to identify if we know what to look for. Although not all false teachers look exactly alike, they tend to display a few common traits that serve as red flags to discerning Christians. First and foremost, they are supremely arrogant. Peter says they are "daring" and "self-willed" and "do not tremble when they revile angelic majesties" (2:10). Commentators debate about who these angelic majesties are, and I encourage you to consider their arguments as you have time. But for our purposes in this lesson, focus on the point that false teachers are characterized by a bold audacity that isn't afraid of or respectful toward anyone.

False teachers also behave like animals who live by sheer instinct. They lack spiritual insight and therefore are motivated, almost entirely, by sensuality. They pursue pleasure and shameless indulgence. Peter describes them as "stains and blemishes" (2:13), the exact opposite of what he says we should be—"spotless and blameless" (3:14).[7] When we encounter a false teacher, we're likely to sense that antipathy and wisely regard it as another red flag.

False teachers tend to be addicted to sin (2:13), although they may be quite good at hiding that fact. They are "trained in greed" (v. 14) having worked long and hard to become experts in avarice. They know what they want—physical pleasures, power, influence, or money—and they pursue their self-styled chief ends with practiced persistence.

Peter also says they are "accursed" (v. 14) and will be destroyed like the unreasoning animals of whom they remind us. That's because they have forsaken "the right way" (v. 15) and walked in the footsteps of the prophet Balaam. Balaam was more interested in prestige and profit than he was in proclaiming God's truth; however, he failed to achieve fame and fortune in the way he desired. Sadly, he has been remembered down through the ages for his willingness to curse God's people for selfish reasons—and for being rebuked by his donkey.

Balaam's sorry example serves as caution and encouragement to believers in Christ. We "do well to pay attention" (1:19) to its warning that selfish pursuits produce nothing of value. And we should draw strength from its reminder that if God can use a "mute donkey" to rebuke a false prophet, He can surely use us!

Peter affirms that false prophets preach hollow messages to those who are most vulnerable to their deception. They target new converts and entice unstable Christians with empty offers of freedom. They do not proclaim the true gospel of freedom in Christ to obey God's commands. Rather, they hold out a license to live, without consequence, apart from God's law. Ironically, the freedom they offer others, they don't have themselves. Peter says these false teachers "are slaves of corruption; for by what a man is overcome, by this he is enslaved" (2:19).

Peter concludes his graphic description of the false teachers among us by reminding us that, no matter how skilled they are in deception, their enslavement to sin will eventually surface.

> For if, after they have escaped the defilements of the world by the knowledge of the Lord and Savior Jesus Christ, they are again entangled in them and are overcome, the last state has become worse for them than the first. For it would be better for them not to have known the way of righteousness, than having known it, to turn away from the holy commandment handed on to them. It has happened to them according to the true proverb, "A dog returns to its own vomit," and "a sow, after washing, returns to wallowing in the mire." (2:20–22)

False teachers may, for a time, look and sound a lot like true teachers. They may, for a time, clean up their lives in alignment with what they know of biblical teaching. However, if their hearts have not been transformed through redemption in Christ, they will not be able to keep it up. They will eventually get entangled with sin and lack the ability to break free of its grip. Like dogs and pigs that behave in accord with their true natures, false teachers can't resist indefinitely the pull of their own depravity. False teachers would be better off if they had never heard the truth of the gospel. The more of God's truth sinners know and reject, the greater will be their condemnation (Hebrews 6:4–12; 10:26–31).

False teachers are doomed, but they're not dead yet. And while they're among us, they will continue to blur the display of God's glory—that is, they will if we fail to take them on. So, pause here before you go on to the exercises to check your grip on the sword of the Spirit. You have an invincible weapon at your disposal. But you must keep it honed and ready for action. Go to God in prayer now and ask Him to kindle within you a greater desire to grow in grace and knowledge of Jesus Christ—so He can use you as effectively as He did Balaam's donkey.

Notes

1. The books of 2 Peter and Jude are very similar, and commentators devote innumerable words to the question, Who borrowed from whom? If you are interested in such discussions, by all means, break out those commentaries and dig into their arguments. For purposes of our study, however, this issue is not of primary concern. Both Peter and Jude warn their readers about the dangers of false teaching in general and concentrate their efforts on helping them recognize and defend against those who proclaim it. Neither Peter nor Jude describes a particular teaching in detail or attempts to refute a particular false teaching point by point. Rather,

they alert Christians to the characteristics of those who teach false doctrine. Peter and Jude are both inspired writers of Scripture who support one another in exhorting believers to take on false teachers.

2. Some commentators say that this verse teaches that genuine Christians can lose their salvation. However, other clear teachings in Scripture affirm the security of our salvation (John 10:27–30; Romans 8:1, 35–39; 2 Timothy 1:12, for example). The wording of 2 Peter 2:1 is admittedly difficult to interpret. But many fine commentators depend on the wise hermeneutical principle of allowing clear passages to shed light on unclear ones. They suggest that the best interpretation of this verse, within the whole counsel of God, is that the false teachers looked, sounded, and represented themselves like genuine Christians but, in fact, were not saved.

3. Dick Lucas and Christopher Green, *The Bible Speaks Today: The Message of 2 Peter and Jude,* ed. John R. W. Stott (Downers Grove, Ill.: InterVarsity Press, 1995), 87.

4. D. Edmond Hiebert, *Second Peter and Jude: An Expositional Commentary* (Greenville, S.C.: Unusual Publications, 1989), 93.

5. Michael Green, *The Tyndale New Testament Commentaries: 2 Peter and Jude* (Grand Rapids: Eerdmans, 1968, 1987), 113, 115.

6. Douglas J. Moo, *The NIV Application Commentary: 2 Peter and Jude* (Grand Rapids: Zondervan, 1996), 157.

7. Several commentators point out that in Greek, "stains and blemishes" (2 Peter 2:13) are exact antonyms of "spotless and blameless" (3:14).

Exercises

Review

1. Read Deuteronomy 18:18–22 and Jeremiah 23:1–32. Based on these passages, define and describe a false prophet. What is the inescapable destiny of a false prophet? How do the false teachers Peter describes in 2 Peter 2 compare with these Old Testament descriptions of false prophets?

2. List several New Testament warnings against false teachers. What common themes run through all these warnings? In your opinion, what is the most dangerous thing about false teachers? Support your opinion with Scripture and careful reasoning.

3. Reread 2 Peter 1:1–21 and briefly describe how *Peter prepares* Christians to take on false teachers before he describes those false teachers. In your own words, explain the wisdom of his approach.

4. Using 2 Peter 2:1–22 and Jude 4–16, paint a word picture of a false teacher. (Be creative if you like—write a poem, a song, a newspaper article, or a short story.)

5. Read Genesis 6:1–9:17; 13:1–12; and 18:1–19:29. Explain in your own words how, in these two instances, God preserved and rescued the godly while keeping the unrighteous under punishment for the day of judgment. What do these two examples tell you about God's sovereignty in all circumstances of life? How do they encourage you?

6. What is a *peirasmos?* How does understanding the meaning of this Greek word help you understand what Peter meant when he wrote 2 Peter 2:9?

Temptation

213

7. What do Jesus' words in Matthew 7:21–23 tell you about false teachers? How will they help you recognize them, pray for them, and take them on?

8. Explain how the example of Balaam is a caution and an encouragement for Christians.

9. How are false teachers like dogs and pigs?

Application

1. Review your memory verses from the previous lesson. Then begin memorizing one or more of the following:

   Ephesians 4:11–16
   Hebrews 4:12
   1 John 4:1–4

2. This week in your prayer time, use Matthew 7:13–27 and Hebrews 4:12–13 to help you thank God for equipping you to recognize and take on the false teachers among us, and to help you seek from Him a deeper desire to grow in His grace and the knowledge of Jesus Christ.

3. D. Martyn Lloyd-Jones affirms that one of the greatest dangers associated with rampant false teaching in the church is that Christians are tempted to succumb to despair and hopelessness. He says, "The power of evil seems so great, so highly organized, so deeply entrenched in life. The whole world seems not only against what we believe, but against God in outlook and practice." Then he points out that Peter does not encourage his readers by saying, "Hang in there. Everything will be OK." Lloyd-Jones reminds us that the Bible "never indulges in light and easy optimism." Rather, it always

comforts and encourages us by way of doctrine (D. M. Lloyd-Jones, *Expository Sermons on 2 Peter* [Carlisle, Pa.: Banner of Truth Trust, 1983], 156–57). Peter, in true biblical form, encourages those under fire from false teachers with the truth of God's sovereign power. The biblical doctrine of God's sovereign power assures us that God is in control (Isaiah 14:24, 27; 46:9–11); He permits evil for His own purposes, which we do not always understand (Deuteronomy 29:29; Isaiah 45:5–7; 55:8–11); and He does not give evil free reign (Job 1:6–11).

Have you ever been tempted to succumb to despair and hopelessness because of the proliferation of false teaching in the church? If so, describe the circumstances that led to this temptation. How did you respond to this temptation? Reflect on your study of 2 Peter thus far and Dr. Lloyd-Jones's comments cited above. How does the doctrine of God's sovereign power comfort and encourage you in the midst of this difficulty (*peirasmos*)? List some specific ways you can respond to such difficulties in the future as opportunities to glorify God instead of as temptations to sin. If you have not been tempted to succumb to despair and hopelessness because of the proliferation of false teaching in the church, how might you use your study of 2 Peter and Dr. Lloyd-Jones's comments to help someone who has been?

4. List several things you have learned in this lesson that will help you recognize false teachers in the church. What are some specific ways you can guard against being influenced by their false teachings?

Digging Deeper

1. John Calvin clearly stated two questions that most serious Christians grapple with sooner or later: "If the Lord

would have his own to be safe, why does he not gather them all into some corner of the earth, that they may mutually stimulate one another to holiness? Why does he mingle them with the wicked by whom they may be defiled?" (quoted in Simon J. Kistemaker, *New Testament Commentary: Exposition of Peter* [Grand Rapids: Baker, 1996], 293). Drawing on what you have learned in this study of 1 and 2 Peter, how would you answer John Calvin's questions?

2. Review your answer to review exercise 1 and read 2 Peter 2:1. Consult good Bible commentaries and other study resources and determine whether there is a difference between false prophets and false teachers. If you determine that there is a difference, describe it.

Primary Passage
2 Peter 3

Supplementary Passages
Genesis 1:1–10
Deuteronomy 32:22
Psalms 1; 90:4
Proverbs 9:7–10; 13:1–3; 16:4
Isaiah 30:30; 34:4; 65:17; 66:15–16, 22
Nahum 1:6–7
Zephaniah 3:8
Malachi 4:1–3
Matthew 24:34–44; 26:31–35
Mark 13:28–37
Luke 22:31–32
Acts 3:19–23; 20:28–32
Romans 2:4; 8:18–25; 9:14–24
2 Thessalonians 2:7–12
1 John 2:18
2 John 7–9

Before reading the lesson material, please read the primary Scripture passage listed above and as many of the supplementary passages as time allows. Then briefly summarize in your notebook what you have read. (Do not go into detail. Limit your summary to a brief description of the people, events and/or ideas discussed in the passages.)

13

The Certainty of God's Promises

God writes with a pen that never blots, speaks with a tongue that never slips, acts with a hand that never fails.
—Charles Spurgeon

Have you ever been tempted to simply forget Christianity and go do something else? Have the sparks generated by your grating witness ever gotten so hot that you didn't think you could take any more? Have you ever been so discouraged, frustrated, frightened, or angered by wolves in the church that you wondered if God really could be in charge of such a corrupt organization? Have you ever struggled with a sense of utter futility in Christian ministry? Have you ever felt like you could have written these clever words I once saw on a tongue-in-cheek greeting card: "It's you and me against the world. . . . And I think we're gonna get creamed!"?

I certainly have. In the twenty-some years since God redeemed me, I've been badly burned by a few flying sparks and deeply hurt by a few well-disguised wolves. There have been times when I've walked away from distressing encounters thinking, *That's it. I'm done. From now on I'm playing it safe and keeping my mouth shut.* There have been times when I've thrown my hands up and wondered where to go to resign. I've been so down, I thought I'd never get up. And I have a hunch that I'm not alone.

The fact is that anyone who determines to stand firm on God's truth and grow in His grace will often be tempted to give in to despair. That's because standing and growing declares war on hell—and hell fights back.[1] Satan despises God's truth and hates to see His glory displayed in the lives of believers. So he attacks with a vengeance, doing all that he can to get us to give up. Standing firm on God's truth and growing in His grace means taking on the world, the flesh, and the devil. Walking worthy of our high calling in Christ clearly is not a stroll in the park on a bright sunny day. It's more like a trek over rocky terrain in severe weather conditions!

Peter knew that fact very well. His worthy walk through this world had born no resemblance to a stroll in the park. He had faced the grim specter of utter despair on at least two occasions (Matthew 14:22–33; 26:75; Mark 6:45–52; Luke 22:61–62). And he may well have considered bailing out at other times in his life. But he was not overcome by those temptations. Why? Because Peter was a product of God's unfailing grace. He knew (for a fact, without doubt) that because of God's grace, giving up isn't an option for believers in Christ. He knew that God always completes the work He's begun (Philippians 1:6) and that His grace is sufficient to sustain us even when we are weakest (2 Corinthians 12:9–10).

The apostle John tells how Peter came face to face with the fact that Christians can't quit—because, by God's grace, they have nowhere to go. Jesus had been teaching some challenging truths regarding the wholeheartedness of Christian commitment (John 6:32–65). Unfortunately, the response of most of His disciples[2] fell far short of wholehearted. John tells us, "As a result of this many of His disciples withdrew and were not walking with Him anymore" (v. 66).

Perhaps even as these pseudo-sheep were walking away, Jesus turned to the Twelve and asked them point blank, "You do not want to go away also, do you?" Scripture doesn't tell us how long they pondered His question, but it does tell us that Simon Peter gave Him their final answer: "Lord, to whom shall we go? You have the words of eternal life. We have believed and have come to know that You are the Holy One of God" (vv. 67–69).

The words of eternal life that cause us to believe in Jesus Christ as Lord and Savior are what keep us in the battle when we'd like to quit. They remind us that although life may be difficult, life without Christ is no life at all. They set our minds on our inheritance instead of our circumstances. And they infuse us with courage and confidence. Standing firm on God's truth and growing in grace is motivated and enabled by the sure hope of His precious and magnificent promises. Peter says if we remember and meditate on what we've been promised, we won't be shaken by mockers. Instead, we'll reflect God's glory well while standing securely on His revelation.

Don't Be Shaken by Mockers
(2 Peter 3:1–10)

Peter wrote his second epistle with the intent of "stirring" his readers, not shaking them. That's why he didn't stop at the end of chapter 2. He seems to have sensed that his vivid description of the false teachers among them could leave them shaken, not stirred—if he didn't go on to remind them again of the sure hope of God's precious and magnificent promises.

As a seasoned leader in the war on God's Word, Peter understood that knowing your enemy is essential. If we want to achieve our common cause of giving God glory, we dare not remain ignorant of our enemy's tactics. However, knowing our enemy can be just as daunting as it is essential. Instead of stirring us to fight manfully onward, it can shake us so badly we're tempted to give in to despair. We face that temptation whenever we get so focused on the enemy's tactics that we lose sight of God's promises.

Peter's closing words in this letter help us fight that temptation. Chapter 2 ends rather abruptly. I picture Peter arresting his scathing denunciation of well-disguised wolves by jerking his quill off the parchment and saying to himself, *Enough about them! Time to get God's perspective on their attack.* He firmly, almost forcefully, turns our attention away from the false teachers, back to the subject he was discussing before taking them on.

> This is now, beloved, the second letter I am writing to you in which I am stirring up your sincere mind by way of reminder, that you should remember the words spoken beforehand by the holy prophets and the commandment of the Lord and Savior spoken by your apostles. (3:1–2)

Peter reminds us that we're holding the sword of the Spirit. We don't have to be shaken by the false teachers among us. All we have to do is tighten our grip on our essential weapon. The true knowledge of God, revealed through the Spirit-inspired prophets and apostles, is our sure defense against sneaky infiltrators. Peter says we are well equipped to take on false teachers. We fight and win by hitting them with the truth.

But we can't hit them with truth we don't know. Peter's admonition to remember the words of the prophets and the command[3] of our Lord spoken by the apostles is, in effect, a clear exhortation to diligent Bible study. The only way we can keep our essential weapon well honed for instant use is by consistently and persistently studying Scripture. Christians who fail to develop good study habits routinely go into battle wielding dull swords. And when we fight with dull swords, we decrease our effectiveness in the battle for truth. Satan loves to see Christian warriors armed with dull weapons. That means he won't have to work very hard to dim the display of God's glory.[4]

Peter obviously didn't want any of his readers facilitating the enemy's nefarious ends, so he did more than exhort us to keep our sword sharp by studying Scripture. He went on to demonstrate how to use that sharp sword in hand-to-hand combat. He cites one of the false teachers' favorite false doctrines and then proceeds to demolish it with biblical truth.

> Know this first of all, that in the last days mockers will come with their mocking, following after their own lusts, and saying "Where is the promise of His coming? For ever since the fathers fell asleep, all continues just as it was from the beginning of creation." For when they maintain this, it escapes their notice that by the word of God the heavens existed long ago and the earth was formed out of water and by water, through which the world at that time was destroyed, being flooded with water. But by His word the present heavens and earth are being reserved for fire, kept for the day of judgment and destruction of ungodly men. (3:3–7)

False teachers know that one of the surest ways to convince us to lay down our weapon is by attacking our hope. That's why they're so quick to target the second coming of

Christ. They know that if they can cause us to doubt Christ's return, they can mangle our living hope of our sure inheritance. So they advise us: "Look around at our world. Its mode of operation hasn't changed since the beginning of time. And it will continue to operate the same way forever. God can't or won't intervene in the natural order of things. Therefore, an event like the promised second coming of Christ, which would disrupt the unchanging natural order of things, is clearly impossible. Only a fool would believe such a thing."

Michael Green says, "Had they been alive today, they would have talked about the chain of cause and effect in a closed universe governed by natural laws where miracles, almost by definition, cannot happen."[5] Of course, that's precisely what modern-day mockers tell you and me. And how do we respond? Do we stop dead in our tracks and immediately lay our sword at their feet in quick concession, muttering something conciliatory like, "Of course, you are right. What was I thinking?" Or do we follow Peter's example and counter false teaching with the true knowledge of God?

Peter's example shows us how the sword of the Spirit, finely honed through deep study of Scripture, deals a death blow to the false teachers' argument. Peter says that God does intervene in the natural order of things. Scripture reveals that He's done it before to accomplish His purposes. And there is no reason to think He won't do it again for the same reason.

Green said that the false teachers' "mistake was to forget that the laws of nature are God's laws; their predictability springs from his faithfulness."[6] And Dick Lucas and Christopher Green remind us that "God is not bound by what we call the 'fixed laws of nature.' "[7] Peter explains that God created the world by His Word using the created agent of water (Genesis 1:2–10). But He did not then bind Himself in submission to the laws of nature that He set in motion.

By the word of His power, God upheld and sustained the

natural order of things through the means He created (Colossians 1:16–17; Hebrews 1:3). And by His word, He also disrupted the natural order of things to execute judgment on sinful humanity (Genesis 6:1–9:17). At His command, the water He had used as His instrument of creation and sustenance was also used as His instrument of destruction. The world that had been created out of water and sustained by water was destroyed through water. And if God can do that with water, He can do it with fire.[8] Only a fool would not believe such a thing.

Following this deft demonstration of how to wield a sharp sword, Peter strengthens his readers with a timely reminder of some deep truth about God.

> But do not let this one fact escape your notice, beloved, that with the Lord one day is like a thousand years, and a thousand years like one day. The Lord is not slow about His promise, as some count slowness, but is patient toward you, not wishing for any to perish but for all to come to repentance. But the day of the Lord will come like a thief, in which the heavens will pass away with a roar and the elements will be destroyed with intense heat, and the earth and its works will be burned up. (3:8–10)

Peter assures embattled believers that God can't be late or "slow" in keeping His promises. He fulfills them according to His eternal schedule, not our earthly one. We get impatient when things don't happen as quickly as we'd like, but God never hurries. He knows those who are His (2 Timothy 2:19) and has decreed that the day of the Lord will not come until they have all come to repentance.[9] He alone knows the time of that day, so speculation and frustration are equally pointless.

However, the fact that the day will bring final judgment

should have a huge impact on our behavior. Knowing that God will keep His promises, in His own time and for His own purposes, spurs us to reflect God's glory well while standing securely on His revelation.

Reflect God's Glory Well
(2 Peter 3:11–18)

For the past several weeks, I have been watching a grim object lesson related to Peter's teaching about Christ's return play out around me. I live in Albuquerque, New Mexico. As I write this, much of New Mexico, Colorado, and Arizona is being destroyed by fierce forest fires burning out of control. Although highly skilled firefighters are doing their best, angry flames fanned by high winds and fueled by drought continue to consume everything in their paths. It has been frightening and grievous to witness, up close, the utter destructiveness of raging fire.

But the destruction I've witnessed here in the Southwest pales in significance when compared with what Peter says will occur at Christ's second coming. Instead of a mere two million acres of forest, a few hundred homes, and a small town or two being devoured by flames, "the heavens will pass away with a roar and the elements will be destroyed with intense heat, and the earth and its works will be burned up" (3:10). But surprisingly, Peter does not find that scenario frightening and grievous. Instead, he presents it as one of God's precious and magnificent promises. He says that contemplating "the coming day of God" should fill us with hope and motivate us to live righteously.

> Since all these things are to be destroyed in this way, what sort of people ought you to be in holy conduct and godliness, looking for and hastening the coming day of God, because of which the heavens

will be destroyed by burning, and the elements will melt with intense heat! But according to His promise we are looking for new heavens and a new earth, in which righteousness dwells. (3:11–13)

The difference between my grim perception of the fires all around me and Peter's hopeful perception of the fires to come has to do with their consequences. The fires around me are purely destructive. But the fires to come are surely productive. The fires around me exchange life and beauty for death and despair. But the fires to come will exchange our fallen world for a new heaven and a new earth, in which righteousness dwells. The fires around me reduce human achievement to smoldering ash and drifting smoke. But the fires to come will refine and reward each righteous effort of God's chosen children.

In short, the fires around me mark the hopelessness of a tragic end, but the fires to come mark the excitement of a new beginning. Green sums up the difference well when he says, "The Christian who is living in touch with Christ can face the thought of the dissolution of all things without dismay—even with joy. . . . In a renewed Universe the ravages of the fall will be repaired by the glory of the restoration."[10]

But the blessed assurance of a new heaven and earth doesn't give us permission to check out of the old heaven and earth just yet. Peter reminds us that being heavenly minded should spur us to do as much earthly good as we possibly can. He affirms once again (as he did in his first letter) that our living hope of our sure inheritance is not a good excuse to drift to the sidelines and coast into heaven. Rather, it is the best incentive to rely on God's grace in daily pursuit of righteous living and powerful testimony.

Therefore, beloved, since you look for these things, be diligent to be found by Him in peace, spotless and blameless, and regard the patience of our Lord as salvation; just as also our beloved brother Paul, according to the wisdom given him, wrote to you, as also in all his letters, speaking in them of these things, in which are some things hard to understand, which the untaught and unstable distort, as they do also the rest of the Scriptures, to their own destruction. You therefore, beloved, knowing this beforehand, be on your guard so that you are not carried away by the error of unprincipled men and fall from your own steadfastness, but grow in the grace and knowledge of our Lord and Savior Jesus Christ. To Him be the glory, both now and to the day of eternity. Amen. (3:14–18)

Peter's final words challenge his readers to pay attention to their conduct and attitudes. They remind us that there is an ineluctable link between belief and practice, conviction and conduct, orthodoxy and orthopraxy. They tell us that God never intended His grace to stop at our salvation; He intended it to also equip us to live for His glory.

Peter describes the new heaven and new earth as the place where righteousness dwells. The word translated "dwell" carries the idea of settling down and being at home. Righteousness is not at home in our fallen world, but it will be in the next. And since this world and its works will be burned up, the only thing we will take with us into the new world is our righteousness. Everything else we possess will be reduced to smoldering ash and drifting smoke.

Scripture teaches that we have two kinds of righteousness: imputed and actual. Imputed righteousness is the righteousness of Christ credited to our account that enables us to enter God's presence as His beloved children (2 Corinthians 5:21; Philippians 3:9; Hebrews 4:14–16). Actual righteousness is our obedience to God's commands.

Both forms of righteousness come to us by God's grace. Imputed righteousness is a free gift of salvation, and actual righteousness is empowered by the work of the indwelling Spirit.

Peter's final words to Christians throughout the ages stir us up to remember that we should work hardest at the things that will last into eternity. They tell us to be diligent to be found by Him "unblemished and spotless," words Peter used to describe Christ in his first letter (1 Peter 1:19). In other words, we should give our best efforts to the pursuit of Christlikeness.

Peter's final words also tell us to "regard the patience of our Lord as salvation" (3:15). In other words, we are to take full advantage of the time we have left to testify boldly of the gospel of Christ. Our efforts will be opposed, just as our beloved brother Paul's writings were twisted and distorted by false teachers for their ends and to their destruction. But we must not be dissuaded by their sneaky assaults. We must not allow them to discourage, frustrate, frighten, or anger us to the point that we give in to the temptation to quit in despair.

We have in our hands the invincible weapon of the true knowledge of God. We can strengthen our grip on the sword of the Spirit by fixing our eyes on God's precious and magnificent promises. God's grace has saved us, but it doesn't stop there. It also sustains us in this world while it prepares us for the next.

Growing in grace and knowledge of our Lord and Savior Jesus Christ will prevent us from falling from our own steadfastness. It will cause us to stand firm on God's truth in the war on God's Word. It will equip us to pursue actual righteousness and bear powerful testimony. It will conform our behavior to our beliefs. And it will give glory to Jesus Christ, both now and to the day of eternity.

And to that we can all say with Peter, *Amen!*

Notes

1. I want to given credit to pastor-teacher John MacArthur for this vivid analogy. Somewhere in one of his books are the words, "When a person becomes a Christian, that person is then and there declaring war on hell. And hell fights back. The faint-hearted and compromisers need not apply." Unfortunately, I have lost track of the specific reference.

2. Bear in mind that the word *disciple* is not synonymous with the word *believer*. The word *disciple* means "learner" and is used here to refer to those who were following Jesus to learn from Him but who may or may not have had saving faith in Him.

3. Commentators speculate about what "the commandment of the Lord and Savior spoken by your apostles" might be (3:2). I tend to agree with those who see it as a general reference to Christ's call to His disciples to "be perfect, as your heavenly Father is perfect" (Matthew 5:48). The apostles spoke this command in their frequent exhortations to believers to pursue Christlikeness in all their behavior.

4. If you have not yet developed sound habits of Bible study, please begin to do so immediately. If you have never learned how to study the Bible, my book entitled *Turning On the Light* may help. You may obtain a copy of this book through your local Christian bookstore or by contacting P&R Publishing, P.O. Box 817, Phillipsburg, NJ 08865 (1–800–631–0094).

5. Michael Green, *The Tyndale New Testament Commentaries: 2 Peter and Jude* (Grand Rapids: Eerdmans, 1968, 1987), 139.

6. Ibid.

7. Dick Lucas and Christopher Green, *The Bible Speaks Today: The Message of 2 Peter and Jude,* ed. John R. W. Stott (Downers Grove, Ill.: InterVarsity Press, 1995), 133.

8. D. Edmond Hiebert explains that when the antediluvian world was "destroyed," it was not obliterated but changed. The antediluvian world "perished" because the continuity of the natural order of things was disrupted and then reconstituted. The world continued to exist, but in a changed condition. It is no longer being sustained by water but by fire. And just as the ancient world was destroyed by the same means God used to create and sustain it, the present world will eventually be destroyed by fire. Hiebert says, "With the coming of the atomic era, it is increasingly clear that the present heaven and earth by their constitution contain the constituent elements for their dissolution by fire" (*Second Peter and Jude: An Expositional Commentary* [Greenville, S.C.: Unusual Publications, 1989], 150). He affirms that these changes in the natural order of things do not take place by "natural law" but by the direct action of God (p. 148). And he assures us that the new heavens and earth will be as different from the present world as the present world is from the antediluvian world (p. 149).

9. Bear in mind that Peter is addressing Christians in this letter. Second Peter 2:8–9 is written to the "beloved"— believers in Jesus Christ—and must be interpreted within that context. God's patience, therefore, should be understood as His attitude toward the elect. The Bible teaches that God does not intend for every member of the human race to be saved (Proverbs 16:42; Romans

9:17-22; 2 Thessalonians 2:11-12; 1 Peter 2:6-8; 2 Peter 2:3-4, 9) but that He will accomplish the salvation of all the elect (Isaiah 43:1-13, 21; John 6:37, 40, 44, 60-65; 17:9, 12, 20-24; Romans 8:29-30). Christ's return awaits the salvation of certain people, chosen by God as His children from before the foundation of the world (Ephesians 1:4; Titus 1:1-3). This is admittedly a difficult doctrine. And if it troubles you, I urge you to investigate honestly what Scripture teaches about it. An excellent resource that will help you do that is James Montgomery Boice and Philip Graham Ryken, *The Doctrines of Grace: Rediscovering the Evangelical Gospel* (Wheaton, Ill.: Crossway, 2002).

10. Green, *2 Peter and Jude,* 154.

Exercises

Review

1. Read John 6:32-69 and use Peter's response to Jesus' question to the Twelve to support this statement: "Giving up isn't an option for Christians because they have no where else to go." Do you see a relationship between Peter's statement in John 6:66-69 and what he wrote in 2 Peter 3? If so, describe it.

2. According to Peter, what prevents us from being shaken by mockers?

3. In your own words, describe how Peter demonstrated how to use what we learn from studying Scripture to answer false teachers. Are you aware of any false doctrines being taught by false teachers now? How might you use what you have learned from your study of Scrip-

ture to explain to your friends and relatives that these teachings are in error?

4. Is it possible for God to be slow or late in keeping a promise? Explain.

5. Describe the difference between my perception of the raging forest fires in the Southwest and Peter's perception of the coming fires that will destroy the earth and its works.

6. How does our living hope of our sure inheritance serve as an incentive to righteous living and powerful testimony?

7. Distinguish between the two kinds of righteousness we possess as believers in Jesus Christ. Explain how they are both dependent on God's grace.

8. Based on what you have learned in this study of 1 and 2 Peter, describe the "ineluctable link" between belief and practice, conviction and conduct, orthodoxy and orthopraxy. (This may be an opportunity for you to learn a few new words. If so, smile, and go get your dictionary.)

Application

1. Review your memory verses from the previous lesson. Then begin memorizing one or more of the following:

   Luke 22:31–32
   Romans 2:4
   2 Peter 3:13

2. This week in your prayer time, use the books of 1 and 2 Peter to help you adore God for His greatness and glory, thank Him for His goodness and mercy, confess

your sins and failures; and to seek from Him the grace that you need to live for God's glory.

3. When God announced the coming judgment of the flood, He gave sinful humankind what amounted to a 120-year grace period. Peter tells us that Noah used that grace period to live righteously and preach righteousness to sinful humankind (2 Peter 2:5). His faithfulness bore the fruit of seven souls who were saved with him in the ark. That may seem like a disappointingly small harvest to us, but those eight believers were obviously those who had been appointed for salvation at that time in history. The period of history in which we now live could also be seen as a grace period of unknown duration (to us), which God is using as part of His means to bring His elect to salvation. What are some of your responsibilities as a Christian living during this grace period? Are you currently fulfilling those responsibilities? If you answered yes, describe how you are fulfilling them and consider how you might fulfill them even more effectively. If you answered no, what changes do you need to make in your daily routine in order to begin fulfilling them? When, where, and how will you make those changes? Who will hold you accountable for following through with your plan?

4. Review the lessons in this study. Then describe, in your own words, how this study has changed your thoughts, attitudes, and actions about Christian living. Give specific examples to illustrate how your thoughts, attitudes, and actions have changed.

Digging Deeper

1. Read Matthew 14:22–33; 26:69–75; Mark 16:7; Luke 22:31–32, 54–62; 24:34; John 21:1–23; and 1 Corinthi-

ans 15:5. Describe the two situations in which Peter was tempted to give in to despair. Although these verses indicate that Peter did yield for a brief time to this temptation, it also reveals that he was not overcome by it. Using what you learned from reading these verses, explain what kept Peter from succumbing to utter despair in these difficult circumstances. (Hint: Pay particular attention to Matthew 14:30; Mark 16;7; Luke 24:34; John 21:7; and 1 Corinthians 15:5.)

2. Michael Bentley affirmed in his commentary on 1 and 2 Peter that Peter's example is a great comfort to those of us who have also failed the Lord grievously. He says, "We are conscious that we have sinned against the Lord and the work to which he has called us. When we consider our behavior we feel sure that there can be no further usefulness for us in God's kingdom. But one of the wonderful things about God's grace and mercy is that he uses failures" (*Living for Christ in a Pagan World: 1 and 2 Peter Simply Explained,* The Welwyn Commentary Series [Durham, England: Evangelical Press, 1990], 159). Consider the biblical accounts of Peter's great failures recorded in the Gospels and the ways that God used him in the early church (see chapters 1–15 of the book of Acts and Peter's epistles). Then describe the comfort we can draw from Peter's example in times of great failure. What does Scripture teach about God's purposes in using failures?

3. Michael Green states in his commentary on 2 Peter and Jude: "Anthropocentric [man-centered] hedonism [belief in pleasure as the highest good and the proper aim of humans] always mocks at the idea of ultimate standards and a final division between saved and lost." Do you agree with him? What are the implications of mock-

ing the idea of ultimate standards? Support your position with Scripture, particularly with truths you have learned from 1 and 2 Peter. Now think about this: John Piper advocates what he calls "Christian hedonism," which is thoroughly God-centered. If you are familiar with John Piper's teachings, explain how his view of hedonism differs from the hedonism to which Green is referring. Why is it important to understand the difference between them?

What Must I Do to Be Saved?

A strange sound drifted through the Philippian jail as midnight approached. The sound of human voices—but not the expected groans of the two men who had earlier been beaten with rods and fastened in stocks. Rather, the peaceful singing of praises to their God.

While the other prisoners quietly listened to them, the jailer dozed off, content with the bizarre calm generated by these two preachers, who, hours before, had stirred so much commotion in the city.

Suddenly a deafening roar filled the prison as the ground began to shake violently. Sturdy doors convulsed and popped open. Chains snapped and fell at prisoners' feet. Startled into full wakefulness, the jailer stared, horrified, at the wide-open doors that guaranteed his prisoners' escape—and his death. Under Roman law, jailers paid with their lives when prisoners escaped. Resolutely, he drew his sword, thinking it better to die by his own hand than by Roman execution.

"Stop! Don't harm yourself—we are all here!" a voice boomed from the darkened inner cell. The jailer called for lights and was astonished to discover his prisoners standing quietly amid their broken chains. Trembling with fear, he rushed in and fell at the feet of the two preachers. As soon as he was able, he led them out of the ruined prison and asked in utter astonishment, "Sirs, what must I do to be saved?"

— — —

In the entire history of the world, no one has ever asked a more important question. The jailer's words that day may well have been motivated by his critical physical need, but the response of Paul and Silas addressed his even more critical spiritual need: "Believe in the Lord Jesus, and you shall be saved, you and your household" (Acts 16:31).[1]

If you have never "believed in the Lord Jesus," your spiritual need, just like the jailer's, is critical. As long as your life is stained with sin, God cannot receive you into His presence. The Bible says that sin has placed a separation between you and God (Isaiah 59:2). It goes on to say that your nature has been so permeated by sin that you no longer have any desire to serve and obey God (Romans 3:10–12); therefore, you are not likely to recognize or care that a separation exists. Your situation is truly desperate because those who are separated from God will spend eternity in hell.

Since your sinful nature is unresponsive to God, the only way you can be saved from your desperate situation is for God to take the initiative. And this He has done! Even though all men and women deserve the punishment of hell because of their sin, God's love has prompted Him to save some who will serve Him in obedience. He did this by sending His Son, the Lord Jesus Christ, to remove the barrier of sin between God and His chosen ones (Colossians 2:13–14).

What is there about Jesus that enables Him to do this? First of all, He is God. While He was on earth, He said, "He who has seen Me has seen the Father" (John 14:9), and "I and the Father are one" (John 10:30). Because He said these things, you must conclude one of three things about His true identity: He was a lunatic who believed He was God when He wasn't; He was a liar who was willing to die a hideous death for what He knew was a lie; or His words are true and He is God.

Lunatics don't live the way Jesus did, and liars don't die the way He did, so if the Bible's account of Jesus' life and words is true, you can be sure He *is* God.

Since Jesus is God, He is perfectly righteous and holy. God's perfect righteousness and holiness demand that sin be punished (Ezekiel 18:4), and Jesus' perfect righteousness and holiness qualified Him to bear the punishment for the sins of those who will be saved (Romans 6:23). Jesus is the only person who never committed a sin; therefore, the punishment He bore when He died on the cross could be accepted by God as satisfaction of His justice in regard to the sins of others.

If someone you love commits a crime and is sentenced to die, you may offer to die in his place. However, if you have also committed crimes worthy of death, your death cannot satisfy the law's demands for your crimes *and* your loved one's. You can die in his place only if you are innocent of any wrongdoing.

Since Jesus lived a perfect life, God's justice could be satisfied by allowing Him to die for the sins of those who will be saved. Because God is perfectly righteous and holy, He could not act in love at the expense of justice. By sending Jesus to die, God demonstrated His love by acting to satisfy His own justice (Romans 3:26).

Jesus did more than die, however. He also rose from the dead. By raising Jesus from the dead, God declared that He had accepted Jesus' death in the place of those who will be saved. Because Jesus lives eternally with God, those for whom Jesus died can be assured they will also spend eternity in heaven (John 14:1–3). The separation of sin has been removed!

Ah, but the all-important question remains unanswered: What must you do to be saved? If God has sent His Son into the world for sinners, and Jesus Christ died in their place, what is left for you to do? You must respond in faith to what God has done. This is what Paul meant when he told the jailer, "Believe in the Lord Jesus, and you shall be saved."

Believing in the Lord Jesus demands three responses from you: an understanding of the facts regarding your hopeless sinful condition and God's action to remove the sin barrier that separates you from Him; acceptance of those facts as true and applicable to you; and a willingness to trust and depend upon God to save you from sin. This involves willingly placing yourself under His authority and acknowledging His sovereign right to rule over you.

But, you say, how can I do this if sin has eliminated my ability to know and appreciate God's work on my behalf? Rest assured that if you desire to have the sin barrier that separates you from God removed, He is already working to change your natural inability to respond. He is extending His gracious offer of salvation to you and will give you the faith to receive it.

If you believe God is working to call you to Himself, read the words He has written to you in the Bible (begin with the book of John in the New Testament) and pray that His Holy Spirit will help you understand what is written there. Continue to read and pray until you are ready to repent, that is, to turn away from sin and commit yourself to serving God.

Is there any other way you can be saved? God Himself says no, there is not. The Bible He wrote says that Jesus is the only way the sin barrier between you and God can be removed (John 14:6; Acts 4:12). He is your hope, and He is your *only* hope.

If you have questions or need any help in this matter, please write to Carol Ruvolo at cruvolo@aol.com before the day is over. God has said in His Bible that a day of judgment is coming, and after that day no one will be saved (Acts 17:30–31; 2 Thessalonians 1:7–9). The time to act is now.

Notes

1. For a full biblical account of this event, see Acts 16:11–40.

What Is the Reformed Faith?

"The Reformed faith"[1] can be defined as a theology that describes and explains the sovereign God's revelation of His actions in history to glorify Himself by redeeming selected men and women from the just consequences of their self-inflicted depravity.

It is first and foremost theology (the study of God), not anthropology (the study of man). Reformed thinking concentrates on developing a true knowledge of God that serves as the necessary context for all other knowledge. It affirms that the created world, including humanity, cannot be accurately understood apart from its relationship with the Creator.

The Reformed faith describes and explains God's revelation of Himself and His actions to humanity; it does not consist of people's attempts to define God as they wish. The Reformed faith asserts that God has revealed Himself in two distinct ways. He reveals His existence, wisdom, and power through the created universe—a process known as natural revelation (Romans 1:18–32); and He reveals His requirements and plans for humankind through His written Word, the Bible—a process known as special revelation (2 Timothy 3:16–17).

Reformed theologians uphold the Bible as the inspired, infallible, inerrant, authoritative, and fully sufficient communication of truth from God to us. When they say the Bible is "inspired," they mean that the Bible was written by God through the agency of human authorship in a miraculous way that preserved the thoughts of God from the taint of human sinfulness (2 Peter 1:20–21).

When they say the Bible is infallible, they mean it is incapable of error, and when they say it is inerrant, they mean the Bible, in actual fact, contains no errors. The Bible is authoritative because it comes from God, whose authority over His creation is absolute (Isaiah 46:9–10). And it is completely sufficient because it contains everything necessary for us to know and live according to God's requirements (2 Peter 1:3–4).

By studying God's revelation of Himself and His work, Reformed theologians have learned two foundational truths that structure their thinking about God's relationship with human beings: God is absolutely sovereign, and people are totally depraved.[2]

Reformed thought affirms that God, by definition, is absolutely sovereign—that is, He controls and superintends every circumstance of life either by direct miraculous intervention or by the ordinary outworking of His providence. Reformed theologians understand that a god who is not sovereign cannot be God, because His power would not be absolute. Since the Reformed faith accepts the Bible's teaching regarding the sovereignty of God, it denies that *anything* occurs outside of God's control.

The Reformed faith affirms the biblical teaching that Adam was created with the ability to sin and chose to do so by disobeying a clear command of God (Genesis 3:1–7). Choosing to sin changed basic human nature and left us unable not to sin—or totally depraved. Total depravity does not mean that all people are as bad as they possibly could be but that every facet of their character is tainted with sin, leaving them incapable and undesirous of fellowship with God. The Reformed faith denies that totally depraved men and women have any ability to seek after or submit to God of their own free will. Left to themselves, totally depraved men and women will remain out of fellowship with God for all eternity.

The only way for any of these men and women to have their fellowship with God restored is for God to take the initiative. And the Bible declares that He has graciously chosen to do so (John 14:16). For His own glory, He has chosen some of those depraved men and women to live in fellowship with Him. His choice is determined by His own good pleasure and not by any virtue in the ones He has chosen. For this reason, grace is defined in Reformed thought as "unmerited favor."

God accomplished the salvation of His chosen ones by sending His Son, the Lord Jesus Christ, to bear God's righteous wrath against sin so that He could forgive those He had chosen. Even though Christ's work was perfect and complete, its intended effectiveness is limited to those who are chosen by God for salvation. Christ would not have been required to suffer any more or any less had a different number been chosen for redemption, but the benefit of His suffering is applied only to those who are called by God to believe in Him.

All of those who are thus effectually called by God will eventually believe and be saved, even though they may resist for a time (John 6:37). They cannot forfeit the salvation they have received (John 10:27–30; Romans 8:31–39).

Reformed thought affirms the clear teaching of the Bible that salvation is by faith alone through Christ alone (John 14:6; Acts 4:12; Ephesians 2:8–9) and that human works play no part in salvation, although they are generated by it (Ephesians 2:10). Salvation transforms a person's nature, giving him or her the ability and the desire to serve and obey God. The unresponsive heart of stone is changed into a sensitive heart of flesh that responds readily to God's voice (Ezekiel 36:25–27) and desires to glorify Him out of gratitude for the indescribable gift of salvation.

Reformed thought affirms that God works in history to redeem His chosen ones through a series of covenants. These covenants define His law, assess penalties for breaking His law, and provide for the imputation of Jesus' vicarious fulfillment of God's requirements to those God intends to redeem.[3]

The Reformed faith affirms that we were created and exist solely to glorify God and denies that God exists to serve us. It affirms that God acts to glorify Himself by putting His attributes on display and that His self-glorifying actions are thoroughly righteous since He is the only Being in creation worthy of glorification. It denies that God is primarily motivated to act by man's needs but affirms that all of God's actions are motivated primarily for His own glory.

The Reformed faith emerged as a distinct belief system during the sixteenth and seventeenth centuries when men like Luther, Calvin, Zwingli, and Knox fought to correct abuses and distortions of Christianity that were rampant in the established Roman church and to restore the purity of the gospel and church life taught by the apostles in the New Testament. Reformed thinkers since their day have sought to align their understanding of God and His actions in history as closely as possible to His truth revealed in the Bible.

Notes

1. This brief overview of basic Reformed beliefs is not intended to be a full explanation of or apologetic for the Reformed faith. For a more detailed description and analysis of the Reformed faith, see R. C. Sproul, *Grace Unknown* (Grand Rapids: Baker, 1997); Loraine Boettner, *The Reformed Faith* (Phillipsburg, N.J.: P&R, 1983); *Back*

to *Basics: Rediscovering the Richness of the Reformed Faith,* ed. David G. Hagopian (Phillipsburg, N.J.: P&R, 1996); William Edgar, *Truth in All Its Glory: Commending the Reformed Faith* (Phillipsburg, N.J.: P&R, 2004); *The Westminster Confession of Faith* (with its accompanying catechisms); or the theological writings of John Calvin, B. B. Warfield, Charles Hodge, and Louis Berkhof.

2. Both of these truths are taught throughout the pages of Scripture; however, the sovereignty of God can be seen very clearly in Isaiah 40–60 and in Job 38–42, while the total depravity of man is described quite graphically in Romans 3:10–18.

3. An excellent discussion of these covenants is contained in chapter 5 of Sproul, *Grace Unknown.*

Recommended Reading

Boice, James Montgomery. *The Doctrines of Grace: Redis-covering the Evangelical Gospel.* Wheaton, Ill.: Cross-way, 2002.

————. *Two Cities, Two Loves: Christian Responsibility in a Crumbling Culture.* Downers Grove, Ill.: InterVarsity Press, 1996.

————. *Whatever Happened to the Gospel of Grace? Recov-ering the Doctrines That Shook the World.* Wheaton, Ill.: Crossway, 2001.

Bridges, Jerry. *The Discipline of Grace: God's Role and Our Role in the Pursuit of Holiness.* Colorado Springs: Nav-Press, 1994.

————. *Transforming Grace: Living Confidently in God's Un-failing Love.* Colorado Springs: NavPress, 1991.

Chapell, Bryan. *Holiness by Grace: Delighting in the Joy That Is Our Strength.* Wheaton, Ill.: Crossway, 2001.

————. *The Promises of Grace: Living in the Grip of God's Love.* Grand Rapids: Baker, 1992, 2001.

Chesterton, G. K. *Heretics / Orthodoxy.* Nashville: Thomas Nelson Publishers, 2000.

Clowney, Edmund P. *The Church.* Contours of Christian The-ology Series. Edited by Gerald Bray. Downers Grove, Ill.: InterVarsity Press, 1995.

Fitzpatrick, Elyse. *Idols of the Heart: Learning to Long for God Alone.* Phillipsburg, N.J.: P&R, 2001.

Hoekema, Anthony A. *The Bible and the Future.* Grand Rapids: Eerdmans, 1979.

———. *Saved by Grace.* Grand Rapids: Eerdmans, 1989.

James, Carolyn Custis. *When Life and Beliefs Collide: How Knowing God Makes a Difference.* Grand Rapids: Zondervan, 2001.

Lloyd-Jones, D. Martyn. *Spiritual Depression: Its Causes and Its Cure.* Grand Rapids: Eerdmans, 1965.

Lundgaard, Kris. *The Enemy Within: Straight Talk about the Power and Defeat of Sin.* Phillipsburg, N.J.: P&R, 1998.

MacArthur, John, Jr. *How to Meet the Enemy: Arming Yourself for Spiritual Warfare.* Wheaton, Ill.: Victor, 1992.

———. *The Power of Suffering: Strengthening Your Faith in the Refiner's Fire.* Wheaton, Ill.: Victor, 1995.

———. *Reckless Faith: When the Church Loses Its Will to Discern.* Wheaton, Ill.: Crossway, 1994.

Murray, John. *Principles of Conduct: Aspects of Biblical Ethics.* Grand Rapids: Eerdmans, 1957.

Packer, J. I. *Rediscovering Holiness.* Ann Arbor, Mich.: Servant, 1992.

Pink, Arthur W. *The Satisfaction of Christ: Studies in the Atonement.* New Ipswich, N.H.: Pietan Publications, 1955.

Powlison, David. *Power Encounters: Reclaiming Spiritual Warfare.* Grand Rapids: Baker, 1995.

Roberts, Maurice. *The Christian's High Calling.* Carlisle, Pa.: Banner of Truth Trust, 2000.

Sproul, R. C. *Grace Unknown: The Heart of Reformed Theology.* Grand Rapids: Baker, 1997.

———. *Surprised by Suffering.* Wheaton, Ill.: Tyndale House, 1988.

Stott, John R. W. *The Cross of Christ.* Downers Grove, Ill.: InterVarsity Press, 1986.

Tada, Joni Eareckson, and Steve Estes. *When God Weeps:*

Why Our Sufferings Matter to the Almighty. Grand Rapids: Zondervan, 1997.

Thomas, Derek. *Taken Up to Heaven: The Ascension of Christ.* Darlington, Durham, England: Evangelical Press, 1996.

Welch, Edward T. *When People Are Big and God Is Small: Overcoming Peer Pressure, Codependency, and the Fear of Man.* Phillipsburg, N.J.: P&R, 1997.

White, James R. *The God Who Justifies.* Minneapolis: Bethany House, 2001.

Carol J. Ruvolo has been teaching the Bible since 1983 and writing books on biblical themes since 1998. A long-time resident of Albuquerque, she now speaks at women's conferences and retreats around the country.

Grace to Stand Firm, Grace to Grow is the seventh in Ruvolo's Light for Your Path series. Among her published works in addition to the series are three studies on the Book of James.

Ruvolo earned B.S. and M.B.A. degrees from the University of New Mexico. Since 1996 she has taken graduate-level courses at Greenville Presbyterian Theological Seminary and several courses from Ligonier Ministries of Canada's School of Theology.

Though a devoted church-goer from childhood, she did not experience God's saving grace until she was an adult. Soon after her conversion she quit her job at a national defense laboratory and began devoting her time to raising her daughter and studying the Scriptures.

During the two years she participated in Bible Study Fellowship, she taught for the first time and soon realized that teaching is her spiritual gift. She says, "I have been teaching, counseling, discipling, and writing about God's revealed truth ever since."

Carol is married and has one child.